DEMOCRACY AT WORK

TRADE UNION STUDIES

Published to accompany a series of programmes
prepared in consultation with the BBC Further
Education Advisory Coucil

Published by the British Broadcasting Corporation
35 Marylebone High Street
London W1M 4AA

ISBN 0 563 16209 0
First Published 1977
© British Broadcasting Corporation 1977
Typesetting by Bishopsgate Press Ltd.
Printed in England by Butler and Tanner Ltd,
London and Frome

This book is set in 10/11 Univers 685

DEMOCRACY AT TRADE UNION STUDIES WORK

A BOOK FOR ACTIVE TRADE UNIONISTS

This book is recommended by the TUC Education Service as a follow up to day-release courses for shop stewards and staff representatives.

This book accompanies the series of ten Trade Union Studies programmes, first shown on BBC 1 at 10.25 a.m. on Sundays starting 8th January 1978, with repeats at 7.05 p.m. on BBC 2 on the following Wednesdays.

The series is being broadcast again on BBC 1 on Sunday mornings, with further repeats at 10.30 a.m. on BBC 2 on Mondays, starting in early October 1978. The weekday daytime showings are for ease of off-air college recording.

British Broadcasting Corporation

Preface

The Trade Union Studies project is a scheme of trade union education designed to help trade unionists in thinking out their own ideas on the policy issues that face them within the trade union movement. The television programmes are accompanied not only by books like this one, but also by new postal courses and study group discussion notes developed by the TUC education service. There are also day schools, study groups and other face-to-face learning opportunities provided by tutors of the Workers Educational Association and the TUC. Thus the project as a whole is the result of collaboration between trade union, broadcasting and educational agencies — one of the first major developments made in line with the recommendations of the Russell Report on Adult Education. The planning has been done by a project team drawn from the Further Education department of BBC tv, the TUC, the WEA, and Sheffield University Extra-Mural Department.

This book is a learning aid specifically designed for trade unionists. Its job is to present its readers with the information and arguments to help them think out their own attitudes and points of view whatever their ideological standpoint within the union movement. It therefore does not itself give support to any particular line of policy or particular union view. It may be important to note that the book was written in the Spring of 1977, and that it reflects the law on employment at that time.

The course content of Trade Union Studies has been developed from an initial overall design by Michael Barratt Brown of Sheffield University Extra-Mural Department. Though based mainly on the work of Ruth Elliott for the TUC Education Service, this book includes contributions by her colleagues Doug Gowan and Andy Fairclough, and by Reg Carnell for the WEA. The book is a joint responsibility of the project team, and like the rest of the BBC's provision to the Trade Union Studies project, it has been made with the full backing of the BBC Further Education Advisory Council.

John Twitchin

Producer, Trade Union Studies
BBC-tv Further Education Department

Contents

How to use this book

If you are studying at home, and really want to get to grips with the course:

1 Read the chapter quickly, to get an overall idea of the subject, and note your answers to the opening questions.

2 Watch the programme (if possible twice).

3 Re-read chapter, noting down your responses to the questions throughout the text.

4 Discuss the issues and action check lists with union colleagues at work.

To get full value, you would also refer back to the two other Trade Union Studies books (see page 181-3). Book 1 lists the main issues for workplace bargaining. Book 2 explains the issues for trade unions about the economy. This Book 3 develops many of the issues raised in Book 1, in taking a closer look at issues of industrial democracy.

It should prove particularly useful to re-read the relevant chapter of Book 1, or to glance over the check lists of issues, just before shop stewards' committee meetings or union branch meetings.

Using the programmes and book in groups

There is no doubt that many trade unionists learn a great deal from group discussion. Your local WEA District Secretary or TUC Regional Education Officer (address page 178) should be able to tell you about classes based on the programmes and this book being offered by tutors in your area.

Many WEA Districts will respond to a request to provide a class on Trade Union Studies for you and your union colleagues (addresses and phone nos pp 178-9).

The programmes can also be used (to obtain them see page 183) to stimulate discussion in more *informal* study groups. You could ask your branch education secretary to set up a discussion group at work; or you could set up a group yourself with the advice of your local union officer. Special discussion notes for such study groups on Trade Union Studies year 1 and 2 are freely available on request from Trade Union Studies, TUC, Tillicoultry, Scotland.

Where no viewing facilities can be arranged, there is no reason why study group members should not meet to discuss the issues, after reviewing the programmes and studying the chapter individually at home. The free copies of the study group notes are designed to help make such discussion useful and effective. A list of the topics and issues covered by the programmes, in case you want to select out only the most relevant, is given on page 181-2.

Some union branches have arranged showings, using films or video cassettes, as a way of encouraging wider participation and debate at meetings. Some trades councils have also taken the same initiative. As a further example, in 1977 the NALGO branch at the LSE used the college equipment to make copies of the programmes and then invited members and representatives from local branches of all other unions to join them in a series of lunch time viewing and discussion sessions. In this way, public service trade unionists in colleges and training establishments with video tape equipment can help make the programmes available to trade union colleagues who don't have such facilities, and discussion of the programme issues can prove an important aid to inter-union joint committee work.

You will find that the Trade Union Studies programmes and this book together provide a full and up-to-date course on ways of extending union democracy. As such, they offer an extra dimension to your union's educational work in helping reps and members to participate better in debate on all the issues involved.

To sum up the ways you could help your union:

1 You can discuss in your local committee or branch how to inform reps and members of the chance to follow the programmes for themselves on TV. (Transmission details are given on the title page.) In any local publicity effort it may be important to add how the programmes only *introduce* the main ideas and issues — the real benefit comes from individual reading of the book chapters. An information job about Trade Union Studies might usefully be done through your local Trades Council or through inter-union meetings in joint committees.

2 You can help draw attention to classes offered by TUC or WEA tutors. You may be able to request the WEA to arrange classes for your colleagues and members.

3 If there are no classes, you could organise a discussion group to talk over the issues raised by the programmes and book chapters. To help lead such discussions you could use the opening questionnaires and the final action check lists from each chapter, as well as the Trade Union Studies discussion notes, free from Tillicoultry.

4 You might ask a local college of further education, or your own union education service, to secure video-cassette or 16mm film copies of the films to use in out of work time discussion sessions for reps and members, based at your workplace, your local college, or union offices.

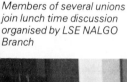

Members of several unions join lunch time discussion organised by LSE NALGO Branch

Chapter 1   Democracy at work — progress report

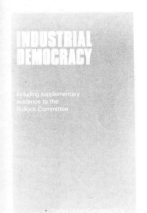

These two quotations raise the key issues for this chapter:

'Throughout their history trade unions have generated a substantial measure of industrial democracy in this country . . . This report recognises that collective bargaining is and will continue to be the central method of joint regulation in industry and the public services . . .'
Opening statement from the TUC's report on Industrial Democracy first published in 1974 and later presented to the Bullock Committee.

'There has already been considerable encroachment into areas which were once considered purely management's domain — such examples are manpower planning, company pensions, and health and safety . . . we view the way forward in the Private Sector as an unlimited extension of collective bargaining, which would ultimately embrace such issues as pricing, long term investment plans, location, forward planning, sales and profitability . . .'
From the 1976 AUEW policy statement 'An investigation into the scope of Industrial Democracy'.

Issues for the chapter

Those quotations raise a number of issues that we will be looking at in this chapter. Many of the issues come up in more detail later in the book. After reading through this chapter you should have clearer ideas on—

1 What the TUC means by 'joint regulation' through collective bargaining.

2 How far there has been 'encroachment into management areas'.

3 Whether there can really be an *'unlimited extension* of collective bargaining' into all areas of decision-making by companies.

First we would like you to answer some questions about collective bargaining as it affects you. Your answers will help you to see how far collective bargaining has developed between your union and your employer. You may also notice gaps that you feel should be filled.

Collective bargaining checklist

1 How far does your employer recognise the union you belong to?
Tick the box that most nearly describes your situation.

☐ not at all
☐ just to represent individual members with grievances
☐ in collective bargaining on wages and basic conditions of employment
☐ in collective bargaining on all aspects of company policy

Yes No
☐ ☐ **2** Does your employer refuse to recognise unions for some grades of employees? (e.g. white-collar staff, part-time workers, etc).

3 Tick the items in the list below which are negotiated between your union and your employer—

- [ ] Basic wage rates
- [ ] Overtime and shift pay
- [ ] Holidays
- [ ] Sick pay
- [ ] Bonus payments
- [ ] Job gradings
- [ ] Pensions
- [ ] Paid maternity leave
- [ ] Recruitment and manpower planning
- [ ] Discipline procedures
- [ ] Disputes procedures
- [ ] Job security agreement
- [ ] Facilities for shop stewards and staff representatives
- [ ] Disclosure of information by management about safety and health issues
- [ ] Manpower
- [ ] Finance
- [ ] Future plans
- [ ] Amount of investment in new plant and machinery
- [ ] Design of new plant and working areas
- [ ] Marketing and pricing of the products you make

As you went down the checklist it probably become less likely that you could tick the boxes. This is not a comprehensive list of all the items you could negotiate about, but it is meant to give you some idea how far collective bargaining has developed in your own situation at work.

Formal and informal agreements

When you were filling in the check list you may have had some difficulty in deciding whether some of the items were the subject of collective bargaining or not. In practice, for example, the union might ask for — and get — information about future plans from the employer, although nothing was agreed in writing. In other words, there might be no formal agreement about the union's rights to information, but informal arrangements (or 'custom and practice') would amount to the same thing.

Some employers may be reluctant to place in writing informal agreements made with unions. This is because some managements like to treat improvements won by the unions as 'concessions' that can be withdrawn; or it may be that a management that reaches agreements on an informal basis with union representatives fears that higher management (or the board of directors) would not approve if it saw written agreements setting out new rights for their employees.

Agreements in the public sector are more likely to be written down in a comprehensive way, although in most public services and industries there is scope for reaching local agreements improving on the national standards.

In this sense, all the later chapters are directly relevant to public sector trade unionists, even where examples and issues are raised in terms of private industry.

👥👥 Have you any personal experience of management being unwilling to reach written agreements when they are willing to go along with informal arrangements?

Do you have ready access to all the written agreements that affect your terms and conditions of employment, and procedures for negotiating with management?

The right to manage

Many trade unionists would say that they should have the right to negotiate about any aspect of employment. But in practice this is rarely the case. While there are managers who accept that control of a workplace in the 1980's means control jointly with the union representatives, other managers will reserve many basic aspects of the way they run their company or service to themselves alone. That is, they will see their job almost entirely in terms of exercising their 'managerial prerogatives', or 'rights to manage'. Even managers who talk of 'management by the consent of the employed' will tend to insist on 'rights to manage' when under pressure, or if disagreements emerge. When trade unionists say they wish to extend collective bargaining, they are really saying that more of the issues that are under management control should be *agreed* between management and unions. You will sometimes see this expressed as *'joint regulation'* of employment questions (which is in contrast to *unilateral* regulation in which control is literally all on one side — the management's).

These illustrations will help you to see the point we are trying to make about extending collective bargaining:

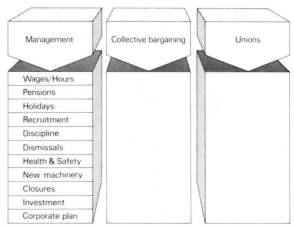

Here management has control over all aspects of work and the running of the company. Unions are not recognised: if the workforce is not organised, it can have no influence over management policies.

This picture was the rule rather than the exception in the nineteenth century. But there are still many patches in British industry where unions are not effectively organised, and where collective bargaining has therefore not been established. We will take up this point later in the chapter.

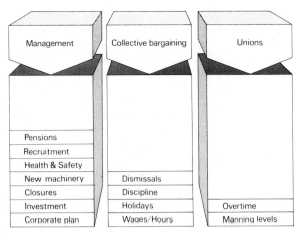

Management	Collective bargaining	Unions
Pensions		
Recruitment		
Health & Safety		
New machinery	Dismissals	
Closures	Discipline	
Investment	Holidays	Overtime
Corporate plan	Wages/Hours	Manning levels

Here some of the management's powers of sole control have been taken away. Wages and conditions of employment have to be negotiated with the unions: and the powers of 'Hire and fire' can no longer be used arbitrarily. The important stage that the unions have reached is to establish the right to object to management decisions as they affect the membership, and to claim improvements in wages and conditions.

But this illustration also makes clear that the fundamental areas of management decision-making about the future of the company — the corporate plan, investment decisions, closures and rationalisations, etc., may remain firmly in management hands. One of the aims of this book is to explore how far unions can influence these big issues at the same time as continuing to make progress on the more bread-and-butter questions.

You will see in the diagram that there is a 'union' box as well as a management box. And of course there can be unilateral *union* control, just as there can be unilateral *management* control, on issues like overtime and manning levels.

In a later chapter we shall be looking at new developments in this area, like experiments in work reorganisation and 'autonomous work groups' which can involve workers in taking on full responsibility for the planning of work (within targets set by management).

Are there any issues in your work place which you feel could be decided by workers alone?

Do you see any problems in workers fully 'taking over' some kinds of management decisions?

Many workers would argue that the real objective of industrial democracy is full unilateral workers control or workers self-management. 'Joint regulation' is just a step on the way to this final objective. In recent years a number of worker controlled co-operatives have been set up and in some of the following chapters we will be looking at what we can learn from their experience about industrial democracy.

Action and Reaction

Unions have always claimed the right to dispute management decisions. In fact many strikes are caused by a union reaction to a management decision taken without consultation or agreement. This struggle between management's right to manage, and the unions' right to dispute decisions affecting their members has been summed up in what has become known as the 'status quo' issue. Bitter struggles have taken place, most notably in the Engineering industry, over the unions' claim that management should not have the automatic right to make changes in working conditions without discussions with the unions.

In 1922 the AEU rejected an agreement containing the clause — 'Instructions of the Management shall be observed pending any question in connection therewith being discussed in accordance with the provisions referred to'.

1922 Engineering lockout: Meeting of AEU members at Coventry

Since one of the main issues in dispute at the time was overtime, and once overtime has been worked it cannot be 'unworked', the bitterness of the unions is easy to understand.

What the union wanted was an agreement that no changes in working conditions could be implemented until *after* the matter had been taken through procedure. A bitter lock-out followed, which the management won. Management reasserted their right to manage and their right to make changes without the prior consent of the unions.

It was not until 1976 that the engineering unions managed to get a status quo provision included in their national agreement — although for a long time before this many managements had *informally* conceded the status quo principle.

This is the model status quo clause recommended by the TUC:

'It is agreed that in the event of any difference arising which cannot immediately be disposed of, then whatever practice or agreement existed prior to the difference shall continue to operate pending a settlement or until the agreed procedure has been exhausted'.

 Does your agreement have a 'status quo' provision?

Using a status quo agreement is an important 'tool' for all trade unionists trying to turn more of the decisions at work into joint decisions.

Consultation or Negotiation?

Unions often claim the right to be 'consulted' about management decisions before they are implemented. And yet 'consultation' may simply mean the management adopting a human face when dealing with the work force in the interests of better morale among employees, and improved co-operation on production planning.

Putting it bluntly, improved consultation could simply be a sort of technique to help management achieve its aims. In that sense it has nothing to do with 'industrial democracy' or an increase in workers' rights; it will probably be concerned with improving efficiency and productivity in industry on their terms alone. Sometimes the phrase 'employee participation' is used to describe this sort of approach. Here is an extract from the CBI's evidence to the Bullock Committee on Industrial Democracy:

'Participation is not an objective in itself. Employee participation is a means of achieving a more competitive, more efficient British industry through improved employer-employee relationships, by ensuring that decision-making in industry is, wherever practicable, with the acceptance of the employees involved . . .'

Among the detailed objectives that the CBI list for employee participation are:

'. . . to ensure that all employees are aware of the reasons for the major decisions which affect them and of the factors taken into account by management in arriving at those decisions; and to ensure that management is aware of the views of all employees before taking such decisions.

. . . to ensure that all employees are aware of the business situation of the enterprise they work for and that they know the nature and extent of the constraints within which it operates.

. . . to inform all employees of the enterprise's forward operating objectives and to provide for discussions of these objectives. . .'

Read over these objectives for employee participation carefully. Do you think they would be effective in extending *joint-decision making* in industry?

The emphasis in such consultative or participation schemes seems to be on the assumption that the relationship between employer and employee is based on co-operation alone, without conflict of interests.

Most trade unionists however, — together with many managers — see that collective bargaining *is* based on a potential conflict of interest in the last resort between employers and employees. They argue that the whole point of getting an independent union organised is to match the strength of the employer. And ultimately the strength of the union has to be based on its ability to take action which could damage the employer's interest — such as a strike or an overtime ban. In the great majority of cases, of course, this type of action is not taken. This is because the negotiations that take place between employers and unions nearly always reach some kind of compromise between the two opposing sides — and some kind of agreement is reached. This is what 'collective bargaining' is all about.

The point of *extending* collective bargaining, as we showed in our illustration earlier, is to ensure that more and more issues that are now regarded as in the area of management's sole control are shifted over to the area of collective bargaining.

A new role for unions

Some people say that 'if unions are really committed to industrial democracy they need to rethink their traditional role'.

We have already seen that the traditional union response is to *dispute* management decisions that affect the membership adversely. But it is management that decides the policy, and makes the decisions.

Look now at what Len Murray has to say about the union role in the future:

'Most importantly, there would be a move away from the negative veto role of resistance to unacceptable management policies, and a shift towards a more constructive approach to policy making and the joint development of alternative strategies and proposals where existing ones seem inadequate. Workers have had enough of just being able to say what they don't want and are now seeking to have a decisive influence over what they do want.'

Len Murray's argument is that unions should move beyond a purely veto role and become much more involved in the process of formulating policy, but some trade unionists have doubts about this approach, and we will be looking at these more carefully in later chapters, particularly when we consider the question of workers on the board. They feel that if unions become too involved in formulating policy, unions will lose their independence. The union and management roles will become mixed up. Unions would find themselves taking on more and more responsibility for planning decisions that might not always be in their members' interests. For these reasons they prefer to stick to a 'veto' role and keep their distance from management.

But it can be argued that the very *objective* of extending industrial democracy is to challenge the idea that there is a separate management

15

function and to insist that more and more issues that are currently regarded as 'management prerogatives' become the subject of joint decision-making. As the 1974 TUC statement on Industrial Democracy says—

'The extension of joint control or joint regulation in any form, including collective bargaining, is a de facto sharing of the management prerogative.'

If unions always stick to a veto role, they are always on the defensive and can never have a positive influence on a policy in the early stages.

On the question of shared responsibility, Len Murray pointed out in his speech to the 1976 Congress that trade unions 'already accept joint responsibility in the case of joint decisions about wages and conditions that have been negotiated through our collective bargaining machinery'. And as all negotiators will know from experience, collective agreements rarely give unions everything they want. They are usually a bargained compromise, reflecting the relative strengths of the two parties at any point in time.

👤👤👤 Can you think of instances where you or your unions have been forced at the end of the day to come to an agreement which you felt gave more to management than to the unions — or vice versa?

The important thing for unions is to develop their organisation and strength to ensure that agreements are as near as possible to union demands. This need becomes even greater as unions try to extend bargaining to long-term policy issues. Union bargaining strength depends in the last resort on the willingness of the membership to back up their demands with industrial action. The problem is that membership support may be strong over bread-and-butter issues such as wage rates, but may fade away over more distant issues that have little immediate impact.

Without being able to rely on strong membership support, worker representatives would be in a weak position to force management to modify their plans, and may be forced to reach a very unsatisfactory agreement.

👤👤👤 Do you think your members would be willing to take industrial action over say management's pricing policy, or over a plan to establish a new factory overseas rather than in Britain?

So far we have outlined in a very general way the basic ideas about collective bargaining and have begun to explore some of the problems raised by extending collective bargaining. It is important that you should try to relate them to your own work place situation and think about how far they apply to you and your union. Many of the issues we have raised run as constant 'themes' throughout the whole book.

We would now like to take up some of the more specific issues or problems about collective bargaining that may have already occurred to you.

Union recognition — is it still a problem?
To some trade unionists studying this book, union recognition may seem to be a matter of history. But this isn't the case: there are probably several recognition struggles being fought at this moment. Sectors in which anti-union employers are still be found include distribution, the financial sector, office employment in general, and small firms in the clothing,

engineering, construction, and general manufacturing industries. If you are a manual worker it may be that the office staff in your own company are not organised into unions and therefore not properly represented for collective bargaining.

The chapter on 'Recognition of Trade Unions' in Trade Union Studies Book 1 (see page 183) gives detailed information on recognition difficulties; more importantly, it lists the issues you may need to discuss in your branch or shop stewards committee on how to help tackle them — whether or not your own union has already got recognition at work.

But for this chapter we need only note that because of the continuing struggle for recognition, a new procedure using the services of ACAS — the Advisory Conciliation and Arbitration Service — was brought in by the Employment Protection Act 1975. This procedure allows ACAS to recommend that a union be recognised by an employer for collective bargaining purposes, after an investigation and possible ballot of sections of the work force has been carried out. The procedure is fully described in a TUC pamphlet 'Recognition', and a free Department of Employment leaflet (available from local job centres). But the new procedure stops short of legal *compulsion on an employer* to negotiate with the relevant union.

The Grunwick Dispute
The case of the APEX dispute over recognition with the film-processing firm Grunwicks demonstrates the limitations of this law. This was the account of the early stages of the recognition element of the dispute, as seen by the APEX union journal:

23 August, 1976. The strike begins. A number of Grunwick employees walk out in sympathy with colleagues dismissed for trivial offences. On the next day they join APEX. As more inside join the union they are harassed by management and so join the strike. Their slogan is "There will be no return to the old conditions". These include basic rates of pay of £25 and £28 for 35- and 40-hour weeks and compulsory overtime. Staff have to raise their hand for permission to visit the toilet. They must take their basic two weeks holiday entitlement outside the peak photographic season, i.e. summertime.

27 August. APEX Senior Area Organiser Len Gristey writes to Grunwick's Personnel Manager seeking talks to resolve the escalating dispute. His offer is rejected.

31 August. By now over 150 employees have joined the union and are on strike, out of a total of about 400 employees, 100 of which are managers and drivers. Many of the strikers and those still at work are students and will soon return to college. APEX asks the Advisory, Conciliation and Arbitration Service to mediate between Grunwick and the union. The company rejects an offer of help from ACAS.

1 September. APEX makes the strike an official dispute for recognition. The following day Grunwick sacks the strikers.

7 September. APEX General Secretary Roy Grantham intervenes in the debate on racialism at the Trades Union Congress in Brighton to draw attention to the dispute. "Here is a clear case," he tells delegates "of a reactionary employer taking advantage of race and employing workers on disgraceful terms and conditions." He details the strike's objectives: "First that the management should recognise the right of all workers to be members of a union. Second, that they should recognise the union of which workers are members. Third, that all those who have been sacked should be reinstated, and that the union should then proceed to negotiate for an end to the deplorable conditions."

23 September. The first of a series of ugly incidents on the picket line takes place. A Jaguar driven by a member of management strikes a woman on picket duty. She is taken to Middlesex Hospital with a leg injury.

15 October. APEX submits a formal claim for recognition to ACAS under Section 11 of the Employment Protection Act. On the same day the strikers march through central London for a lobby of Members of Parliament. At a meeting in the Palace of Westminster local MPs Reg Freeson and Laurie Pavitt speak in support of the strike. In vain ACAS tries once again to persuade the company to co-operate in conciliation talks with the union.

1 November. Members of the Union of Post Office Workers start to black all Grunwick mail. In addition deliveries of materials to the company have dried up thanks to blacking by trade union members employed by suppliers. The postal ban is debated on the next day in the Commons. Minister of State at the Department of Employment Harold Walker slams the company for not co-operating with ACAS. Meanwhile outside the company's Chapter Road works police arrest eight pickets who are charged with obstruction of the highway.

4 November. Backed by the extreme right-wing pressure group, the National Association for Freedom, the company prepares an injunction to have the postal ban lifted. But with work at a standstill Grunwick agrees to co-operate in an ACAS inquiry. In response the UPW lifts its mail boycott.

11 November. Some 100 MPs put their names to a Commons motion deploring the working conditions of Grunwick and expressing dismay that only after industrial pressure did it agree to co-operate with ACAS.

12 December. At a strike meeting in Willesden TUC General Secretary Len Murray pledges his full backing for the strikers' cause. On the following day Grunwick's Managing Director, George Ward, in an interview with a North London newspaper boasts, "APEX are out. They can do what the hell they like." On ACAS he comments "ACAS as constituted under the Employment Protection Act is to encourage collective bargaining. That means trade unions. I do not think you could call them impartial." A week later in an Adjournment Debate in the House of Commons Ted Fletcher MP (Darlington) warns, "if the firm is successful in delaying a ballot through procrastination, this will destroy the intention of Section 11 of the Employment Protection Act, and it will be a signal for other firms to follow the lead that this firm has given."

29 December. ACAS sends out questionnaires to all the APEX members including some still working inside the factories. Other Grunwick employees are denied the opportunity of giving their opinion on the issue of union recognition as the company has failed to provide ACAS with facilities to seek their views. This follows nearly two months of consultations between ACAS and the company in which Grunwick has raised one legal objection after another to the inquiry. The company has insisted that all workers including drivers, warehousemen and managers should be included in the ballot, and not just the groups for which APEX is seeking recognition. Grunwick has objected to the strikers being included in the ballot and to APEX being named on the questionnaire. ACAS is convinced that the company will never co-operate in the inquiry, so it presses on with the ballot without the company's co-operation.

14 January, 1977. The strikers march through Willesden and are joined by groups of local trade unionists. About this time they begin picketing of chemist and photographic shops retailing Grunwick films. Considerable success is achieved and some sixty outlets in the London area stop using the company's products.

10 February. ACAS issues a draft of its report on the recognition claim. It recommends that the company should recognise APEX. To the question "Do you want the Association of Professional, Executive; Clerical and Computer Staff (APEX) to negotiate with your employer about your pay and conditions of employment?" the answer ·"Yes" is given in all 93 forms returned. The following week Roy Grantham writes to George Ward offering talks. This offer is subsequently rejected.

24 February. Six of the pickets arrested on 1 November are found guilty of causing an obstruction to the highway. Roy Grantham describes the verdict as "a threat to the fundamental right to picket peacefully." The union decides to support an appeal.

9 March. On the day the final ACAS report is published four more pickets are arrested and charged with obstruction of the highway.

11 March. Worried by its loss of trade after scores of shops have stopped using Grunwick film, the company tries unsuccessfully to win an injunction preventing the picketing of chemists.

23 March. The TUC General Council issues a statement, circulated to all affiliated unions, asking trade unions to black all Grunwick supplies, to urge a boycott of Bonuspool and Trucolour films and to give financial assistance to the strikers. On the same day an industrial tribunal rejects on a legal technicality applications for unfair dismissal by Grunwick from a number of the strikers.

12 April. With the start of the peak film processing season, picketing is intensified around the factories. Picket lines are manned 24 hours a day, seven days a week at the company's six entrances.

19 April. A High Court writ is served on behalf of Grunwick challenging the ACAS report. The writ seeks to have the report declared *ultra vires* and void.

27 April. Labour MPs lead a march of fourteen hundred strikers and supporters through Willesden. At a rally after the march Roy Grantham warns, "Either this company moves into the Twentieth Century or it should go out of business. Either it agrees to negotiate, or it goes out of business."

3 May. The appeal from the six pickets convicted is upheld in Middlesex Crown Court. The police must pay costs. Thus a vital trade union principle of peaceful picketing is successfully defended.

The question for trade unionists is: can they rely on the law being properly implemented to guarantee their members rights? The Grunwick story — even *before* the mass picketing support that hit the headlines in June 1977 — suggests to many trade unionists that trade union organisation and solidarity remain necessary if workers are to win and retain any rights at all in practice.

And of course there are various *degrees* of recognition. Management may recognise a union's right to negotiate over wages and basic conditions, but may refuse to recognise the union's right to negotiate on overtime working, or health and safety, or to give union stewards proper facilities to do their jobs. So recognition battles are likely to become more and more important as unions fight to extend collective bargaining beyond wages.

Hasn't the law helped to improve workers' rights without the need for collective bargaining?

Not entirely. The new employment rights won by unions through legislation such as the Employment Protection Act really depend on trade union organisation to be implemented. This point is dealt with more fully in later chapters, when we deal with issues to do with Health and Safety, Equal Pay and Sex Discrimination, Pensions, Disclosure of Information, and Facilities for Union Representatives. But here are some general points we will keep coming back to throughout the book:

Legislation is no good unless its enforced

Having a legal right is one thing: enforcing it is another. Often only an effective union organisation can make sure that an employer does not ignore the spirit of his legal obligations. Although there are legal minimums for wages in some low-pay industries (such as catering) for example, without union organisation it is all too easy for employers to dodge the regulations.

The law provides only minimum standards

Many law-based employment rights are skeletons which only take proper shape when filled out by collective agreements. In the next chapters there are several examples of unions using the law to build significant improvements — maternity leave and maternity pay are good examples. (Chapter 4).

The big steps forward in industrial democracy and workers rights have been fought for through negotiation. Sometimes these negotiated rights become legal rights. But the best organised workers are always a long way in front of the law.

Could Collective Bargaining be extended to cover all aspects of company operations – including investment, manpower, and pricing?

This is a difficult question to answer. If you look back to the AUEW policy statement quoted at the beginning of this chapter you will see that it is certainly a union *aim* to extend collective bargaining to the highest levels. But in practice this is rarely achieved at the present time.

Unions will reserve the right to *react* to company decisions about investment policies and future planning in general. This is especially true where jobs are threatened. But it is difficult for unions to make positive claims to management about their planning policies. Most unions are still in a 'veto' position whether they want to be or not. One of the reasons for this is that many fundamental decisions are taken at boardroom level, rather than at lower levels of management. Decisions to close a whole plant, to open a new line of production, or to switch investment abroad, would certainly be taken by the company directors. Unions rarely have prior access to information about this sort of company decision.

Another factor is that in private industry collective bargaining often takes place in individual *plants* or *sites*, as well as at the level of the whole *industry*, but employers refuse to negotiate at *company* level. This places a very significant limitation on negotiations. Although wages and conditions of employment may be negotiated plant-by-plant up and down the country, issues which affect the company as a whole simply *cannot* be negotiated. So any question of collective bargaining about the big issues of investment and manpower planning falls into abeyance, unless new collective bargaining machinery can be established at company level. And this means that trade unions need to develop their own company-level organisation. This issue is looked at in detail in Chapter 6.

A final point is that there are some issues of vital importance for workers — like mergers — that could never be fully resolved in negotiations with management. Because the last word here rests with the shareholders or owners of the companies involved. In other words, unions are up against *owner prerogatives* as well as management prerogatives. We look at this issue again in Chapter 7.

Workers from Parsons, Newcastle protest against a proposed merger with G.E.C.

Getting the information we need

You will find that every chapter of this book has a questionnaire at the beginning which asks you about the situation of your work place. Sometimes you may not have the information available and it may take some time and effort to hunt it out. But all the information referred to is information you *ought* to have on a regular basis from management. By the end of the book you should have a much clearer idea about the kinds of information you need if you are to extend union influence and joint control in your company, and in the last chapter we look at the idea of *information agreements*. We also look there at the kind of training shop stewards need so that they can really use this information.

Action checklist

● Carry out a review of trade union organisation in your company/service, and in your locality, based upon questionnaire (pp 9-10).
● Make sure you have a complete collection of all collective agreements affecting your conditions of employment.
● Discuss in your branch or shop stewards committee your priorities for improvements in
— wages and conditions of employment.
— trade union rights, facilities and procedures.

Join the Protection Gang

wear protective footwear!

THIS ISN'T A SITE FOR SORE EYES!

WEAR PROTECTIVE GOGGLES

SAFE IMPACT

Chapter 2   Get Organised — for Safety's Sake!

We saw in Chapter One that the extension of Industrial Democracy must be based on the development of trade union organisation and involvement — to give workers a greater say over more areas of decision-making at work. It was also suggested that unions should have more positive influence in decision-making and planning, instead of just reacting after management had made up their minds to do something. This chapter reviews these objectives in more detail by looking at the implications of greater trade union involvement in decisions affecting health and safety at work.

Issues for the Chapter
1 How should trade unions improve their organisation at the workplace so as to have more say on health and safety matters?

2 How can trade unionists get information about substances and machinery used at work so that everyone is aware of the hazards they work with?

3 What part does the law play in developing greater safety at work?

4 How can trade unionists make the best use of the Health and Safety at Work Act and the new regulations on safety representatives and safety committees?

Questions
Before working through the chapter or watching the television programme, note down your answers to the following questions:

Yes No

☐ ☐   **1** Does your employer have a safety committee to discuss health and safety issues arising in your workplace plant or company?

☐ ☐   **2** Do trade unionists sit on this safety committee?

If they do, how are they appointed?

☐ ☐   **3** Is there a management majority on the safety committee?

      4 Does the committee discuss the following matters —

☐ ☐   hazards or incidents which have occurred recently

☐ ☐   quarterly accident and sickness figures

☐ ☐   results of inspection and Factory Inspectorate visits

☐ ☐   accident prevention programmes

☐ ☐   employee instruction and training

☐ ☐   developments in fire/evacuation/emergency procedures

☐ ☐   expenditure on health and safety programme improvements

☐ ☐   the provision of correct safety equipment and protective gear

5 Do trade unionist representatives at your workplace receive information on —

Yes No

☐ ☐ changes to plant, equipment and materials which could have effects on safety

☐ ☐ technical information about the hazards at work

☐ ☐ records of accidents, diseases and sickness

☐ ☐ results of measuring the work environment

☐ ☐ **6** Do trade union representatives at your workplace regularly discuss matters of health and safety?

☐ ☐ **7** Do you have agreed arrangements with management for dealing with health and safety at work, including arrangements for disclosure of information?

☐ ☐ **8** Does your employer have a written safety policy?

Hazards at work
Chapter 6 of the year one Trade Union Studies book was about health and safety at work. If you have a copy, you will find it useful to review that chapter before reading on.

We need to recall some of the issues which were raised in that previous chapter. The following questions are particularly important.

Why do accidents and ill-health occur?

Accidents may not happen every day at your workplace but when they do, people may tend to say they are caused by something the victim was 'doing wrong' — perhaps having an 'off day', not 'looking out', or 'being careless'. But this explanation may *not* actually account for all accidents and cannot account for many diseases contracted at work.

In fact every accident involves both an individual and a work situation with its own dangers. Employers are under an obligation to reduce risks and hazards, and trade unionists should not be content with management solutions which depend only on workers adapting better to existing conditions at work.

A trade union view on health and safety at work should be concerned not just about whether workers are careful and responsible in their attitude to safety procedures. It should be concerned with reducing risks by intervening in the design of the production process at an early stage, and by seeking to ensure that hazardous equipment and work practices are made safer.

This clearly would mean greater union involvement in the analysis of accidents and ill-health at the workplace, and in management planning and purchasing decisions.

This may not be as easy as it sounds. It may be hard to pin down precisely where the relevant decisions are made.

 Who made the decisions to buy and use the equipment and materials you use at work?

Were you or your union consulted about the safety aspects of changes in these materials and equipment?

Who designed the layout of your factory shop floor, office or place of work?

If you don't know the answers to any of these questions, how would you go about finding out?

Even if you know who makes these decisions, it may be hard to exert influence on them. If you try to discuss questions of equipment purchase or plant design with managers at plant level, you may find that they can't really give any firm decisions — these questions may be decided higher up the organisation at company level.

If decisions are made at company level you may not have adequate company level trade union machinery.

The company may refuse to bargain at the higher levels of decision-making.

Even where management and workers agree that safety problems need to be tackled, they may still disagree on how to improve things.

Here is an example:

Management may want to solve problems caused by fumes by issuing respirators and protective clothing. Trade unionists might prefer that adequate ventilation systems were installed, or that safer chemicals be used in place of poisonous ones, in order to reduce risks. This example illustrates that there are a range of possible solutions for health and safety problems. Worker representatives should press for those solutions which give their members most protection — not necessarily the solution put forward by the employer.

Health and safety and the law

In the past, health and safety matters at the workplace have been regulated by factories and allied legislation, supervised in most cases by the Factory Inspectorate.

But with less than a thousand inspectors and over one million workplaces (which means one factory inspector per 17,000 workers) Factory Inspectors have had difficulty in covering detailed working arrangements in all factories.

Furthermore, most breaches of the law did not result in prosecution, and fines levied were quite low, around £100 for the offences which actually resulted in prosecution.

The TUC and many other unions since the mid nineteenth century have consistently pressed for an expansion of the factory inspectorate and for stiffer fines on prosecution.

Because the main source of pressure for safer work has always been the trade union movement, and because the 'front-line' job of ensuring safe work can only be done on the shop floor, more and more trade unionists are seeing that the key to safer work is better union organisation. The new Health and Safety at Work Act recognises for the first time in law (apart from the special case of coalminers) that unions and their members have a fundamental part to play. Sections of this Act provide for new developments in trade union organisation at work. As a result unions will need to become more involved in

identifying hazards and dangers

influencing management decisions

developing and enforcing standards of safe work

The rest of this chapter should help you think about trade union strategies for improving health and safety at work. It deals with these issues:

1 Trade union organisation

2 Information about safety

3 Procedures for dealing with management

4 Safety agreements

Each section will give details of the laws and regulations which could help to develop union organisation.

(We do not try to cover all the aspects of the Health and Safety at Work Act which were discussed in Year One of Trade Union Studies).

Trade union organisation and safety

Union objectives

There are three main objectives for unions wishing to organise better on safety matters and reduce hazards:

To develop a stronger system of *representation* for safety issues

To ensure that safety receives a *higher priority* in union policies

To develop *membership awareness* about safety by giving more information and leadership from the union. This will strengthen the union in negotiations with management over safety.

The law and union organisation

One of the most significant features of the Health and Safety at Work Act is that it provides legal support for developments in union organisation. The regulations which give details of this section of the Act are available in the booklet 'Safety representatives and safety committees'. This is published by the Health and Safety Commission. (It is available from Government bookshops, or through your union).

These new regulations come into force in October 1978. The law will provide support to unions in seeking to improve union organisation, but it will still be up to unions to a great extent to make sure that the regulations are used in the best way.

The regulations say that —

Safety representatives can be appointed by independent trade unions which have been recognised for bargaining by the employer.

The unions have the right to decide the trade union procedures to be used in the selection of safety representatives.

Trade unions have the right to decide how many safety representatives are needed, and which areas they should cover.

Normally, safety representatives must be employees. Where possible they should have been working for their employer for at least two years.

Functions of safety representatives

For safety representatives the Regulations give rights —

to investigate potential hazards whether or not they are drawn to his attention by the people he represents

to investigate dangerous incidents

to examine the causes of accidents

to investigate complaints by any employee he represents relating to that employee's health, safety and welfare at work

to make regular routine inspections of their area of responsibility at least every three months, and more frequently where this is agreed with the employer

to receive information from the Factory Inspectorate

These functions will assist the development of trade union influence over

Health and Safety at Work

Safety representatives and safety committees

This booklet contains the proposals for regulations and an approved code of practice under the provisions of the Health and Safety at Work etc. Act 1974 as finally agreed by the Health and Safety Commission and submitted to the Secretary of State for Employment. It also contains guidance notes based on these proposals.

Health and Safety Commission

I'M WORRIED ABOUT THE GUARDS ON MY MACHINE

GET THE UNION SAFETY REP TO TAKE A LOOK. HE'LL TAKE IT UP.

safety and health matters. One vital point to be aware of is that the Guidance Notes accompanying the Regulations say explicitly that —

'a safety representative, by accepting, agreeing with or not objecting to a course of action taken by the employer to deal with a health or safety hazard, does not take upon himself any legal responsibility for that course of action'.

In addition safety representatives would have a right to certain facilities to help them to do their jobs —

time off work with pay (at average earnings) to enable representatives to deal with safety matters

time off with pay to attend training courses approved by the unions

assistance from management in performing safety inspections

access to information from management

Checking on noise levels

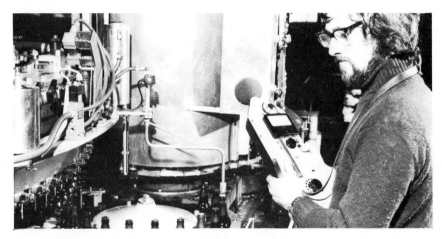

Issues for union policy

These Regulations give trade unions the right to appoint safety representatives at the workplace. But unions will still need to develop policies for trade union safety organisation.

Firstly, although the Regulations do not come into effect legally speaking until October 1 1978, unions will not want to delay entering into discussions with employers about implementing the Regulations during the lead-in period.

Secondly, within the framework of the regulations, there are certain options and choices for unions which they will have to decide for themselves.

On certain items, for instance facilities for safety representatives, or for information, unions may wish to go beyond the minimum standards laid down in the regulations.

Here are some examples of policy decisions which unions will have to make.

a Should safety representatives be shop stewards?

If safety representatives were shop stewards, they would be accountable to their members within existing union rules and procedures

They would be more able to deal with safety as part of the normal business of industrial relations, not as a separate issue unrelated to other union concerns

There would be established procedures within the unions for safety representatives to relate to each other, and discuss safety items through the system of stewards committees

Where safety considerations appear to conflict with other issues, for instance bonus earnings, or job security, then this would not give rise to a clash between steward and safety representative.

On the other hand, where shop stewards are already overworked — or where hazards at work are particularly complex, or specialised, then there may be a case for having safety representatives who concentrate on safety matters only.

 Do you think that safety representatives at your workplace should be stewards or specialists?

Does your trade union have any national policies on this issue?

If safety representatives were specialists, can you think of any safeguards to prevent safety matters being separated off from other aspects of trade union business?

Here is one suggestion put forward by the TUC:

'In areas where shop stewards committees or joint representation committees exist, it may be advisable to establish safety representatives within the existing shop steward structure. For example, a safety representative sub-committee under the parent shop steward committee'.

b How can unions increase members' interest and involvement in safety matters?

One approach might be to negotiate an agreement with management to permit workplace meetings of members to discuss safety and other matters. Some might be able to show the TU Studies films on health and safety at such meetings, to stimulate discussion of issues raised in the book chapters (for films see pp 183). But in any case, under the Health and Safety at Work Act, management will be obliged to pass on information about safety and health and it is important that members should discuss this information at trade union meetings.

c What facilities should be provided for safety representatives?

Trade unions will need to negotiate with management about facilities for safety representatives. As well as the facilities specified in the regulations, others as such as office space, use of 'phones, noticeboards, meeting rooms and access to office or training dep't facilities may be useful.

d Functions of safety representatives?

The prime objective of union policy here must be to ensure that all safety representatives are aware of the functions laid down for safety representatives in the regulations and use them to the full. To achieve this would be a big step forward. Think for example about the function of 'investigating potential hazards whether or not these are drawn to his attention by the people he represents'. This gives a safety representative the opportunity to investigate the relevant area of his workplace at any time, not just on the occasion of three-monthly inspections, and to take up with management not only hazardous situations that have caused accidents or near accidents, but also any work practice which the safety representative in his opinion feels could be hazardous at some point in time.

While implementing the regulations must be the first objective, there is no reason why unions should not ultimately seek to build on the provisions of the Regulations.

For example, they might get an undertaking from management that formal inspections could take place more frequently than at three monthly intervals where this was justified.

Information on safety at work

Information — trade union objectives

Safety representatives and shop stewards (often the same person) will need adequate information about existing health hazards. They will also want to know about any proposed changes which might affect safety and health — for example, the introduction of new machinery or the use of new chemicals. They will want information from employers, from the Factory Inspectorate, from published booklets and studies, from their unions and from other sources. Having got the information, safety representatives and shop stewards will need to interpret and use it. This raises the question of training for safety representatives and of procedures for dealing with management.

Information and the law

The Health and Safety at Work Act and the new regulations contain new rights for safety representatives to receive information about safety from several sources:

Management

The Code of Practice in the 'Safety Representatives and Safety Committees' booklet defines the kinds of information which workers ought to receive from management. Look back to question 5 of the beginning of the chapter. All the types of information listed here are referred to in the Code of Practice.

 How much of this information do union representatives at your workplace already receive?

The law requires each employer to publish a policy statement on health and safety at work. The Health and Safety at Work Act says that employers must bring this policy statement to the notice of employees.

The Health and Safety Commission Guidance Note on 'Employers' policy statements' advises that the policy statement should specify in detail the people on the management side who are responsible for making particular decisions involving health and safety. This may help unions to find out where decisions are made on the management side.

The Health and Safety Executive

The Health and Safety Executive is an amalgamation of all the various Inspectorates, including the Factory Inspectorate, which had the job of enforcing health and safety law before the Health and Safety at Work Act.

Safety representatives will have certain legal rights to obtain information from factory and other inspectors in connection with inspectors investigations, and information about what the inspector proposed to do as a result of investigations. Factory inspectors may also provide technical information and help if workers encounter problems.

Other Sources
Manufacturers of equipment and substances for use at work are obliged, by law, to provide information about the safe use of their products, and the results of any tests they have carried out.

Information — issues for union policy
Again the first objective must be to make sure that safety representatives are fully aware of what the Regulations say about information. The code of practice accompanying the Regulations refers only to broad kinds of information.

Trade union representatives may find it helpful to agree with management about the precise kinds of information which they require. These might include certain management documents, safety consultants reports, accident and illness records, details of expenditure on health and safety, insurance under-writers reports and manufacturers literature on machines and substances.

 Does the union get any of this information at the moment?

It might also be established in an agreement that management should provide documents such as Acts of Parliament, Regulations, Codes of Practice, standards and reports relevant to your work-place.

We return to the question of information agreements in chapter 10. You may also find it useful if your stewards committee and union locally collects a small library of information, agreements and source books on safety at work, in addition to the items listed above.

HEALTH SAFETY

Procedures for raising safety issues with management

Trade union objectives
When considering setting up procedures for handling safety matters, unions will have a number of objectives in mind:

a to ensure that procedures operate without delay
b to provide for urgent items to be taken up immediately
c to ensure that safety matters are not divorced from normal union business.

In many workplaces these objectives might best be met by dealing with safety matters through existing trade union-management procedures. Unions may decide however, in some situations, that a special safety committee consisting of safety representatives and management representatives would assist in handling safety issues. In some workplaces safety committees may exist already and trade unionists may want to decide in the light of the new Regulations whether these need reviewing.

Dealing with management — the legal position
After October 1978 safety representatives will have the right to make representations to their employer about particular complaints and grievances or about more general problems of safety and health.

This is what the Guidance Notes accompanying the Regulations have to say on this point:

'It is important that safety representatives should be able to take matters up with management without delay. They must therefore have ready access to the employer or his representatives; who those should be will be determined in the light of local circumstances. It may not be desirable to specify one individual for all contacts, bearing in mind that hazards could involve differing degrees of urgency and importance. The need is to ensure that safety representatives have a clear idea as to who is authorised to act as the employer's representative for the purpose of thse Regulations'.

If two or more safety representatives request it, the employer must establish a committee to discuss safety issues. But the decision is up to the safety representatives. There is no legal stipulation that safety committees must be set up. Where they are set up, the Guidance Notes accompanying the Regulations state that the membership and structure of safety committees should be settled in consultation between management and the trade union representatives concerned through the use of normal machinery.

The 'Guidance Note' recommends that:

'The number of management representatives should not exceed the number of employees representatives',

and that management representatives should include people with 'adequate authority to give proper consideration to views and recommendations'. It is important to note that the law will oblige employers to listen to representations from safety representatives, whether they are channelled through a safety committee or not.

Trade Union Policies on Safety Committees

Many existing safety committees are little more than consultative bodies with no power to take decisions. In this situation effective and decisive action on health and safety matters might more easily be achieved by direct negotiations between safety representatives and the relevant managers. On the other hand, safety committees can perform a useful function if they have adequate powers, and trade unionists might want to use the opportunity of the Regulations to make existing safety committees more effective.

Here are some issues you will need to think about if you are considering establishing or overhauling a safety committee at your workplace.

Composition of safety committees

Unions will want to make sure that:

as recommended in the Guidance Notes, at least 50% trade union representation is achieved

as recommended in the Guidance Notes, as senior a manager as possible is chairman. (The managing director or deputy chairman if possible — someone, with real authority to make decisions). Ideally the chairman should deal with safety budgets for the company

the trade union side of the safety committee should be able to meet independently of management before safety committee meetings

the safety committee should have access to all company information which has a bearing on health and safety at work

the safety committee should have the power to discuss all matters which have a bearing on health and safety at work. (Look back at the points listed in question 4 at the beginning of the chapter. These are all matters that safety committees should discuss) unions will want to ensure that the trade union side of safety committees remains accountable to existing trade union workplace organisation.

 Can you think of any other policies which would improve safety committees from the unions' point of view?

Does your present safety committee conform with the policies outlined above?

You will also need to consider whether one safety committee is adequate for an organisation as a whole, or whether more are needed.

Read the following extract from the Guidance Notes and decide your own answer to the question below.

'Safety committees are most likely to prove effective where their work is related to a single establishment rather than to a collection of geographically distinct places. There may be a place for safety committees at group level for larger organisations; this will apply where relevant decisions are taken at a higher level than the establishment. In general, it should be unnecessary for an employer to appoint duplicate committees for the same workplace, e.g. representing different levels of staff. In large workplaces, however, a single committee may be either too large, or if kept small, may become too remote.

In these circumstances, it may be necessary to set up several committees with adequate arrangements for coordination between them.'

Safety Representatives and Safety Committees, Health and Safety Commission

 If you have a safety committee system in your organisation do you think the number and level of committees is right?

Safety Agreements

One way forward is to negotiate with management for a comprehensive safety agreement incorporating and building on all the basic points in the safety representatives/safety committee Regulations.

General points to consider when doing this might be:

how can the agreement be used to strengthen union organisation?

how can the provisions of the regulations on safety representatives and safety committees be built upon and extended?

Specific matters to be taken up in negotiations might be –

1 Function of safety representatives

2 Procedures for conducting safety representatives inspections

3 Facilities for safety representatives

4 Provision of information

5 Procedures for taking up safety grievances

6 Structure and function of safety committees

7 Training provisions for workers and supervisors. Union training for safety representatives.

Collective bargaining and safety at work

This chapter has discussed the development of union organisation and the extension of collective bargaining into new areas. These are fundamental parts of the campaign for greater industrial democracy. But we need to ask whether the extension of collective bargaining can always provide the degree of increased influence which workers seek. Management decisions with implications for safety might be taken in situations where the possibilities for bargaining were limited or non-existent.

An example which illustrates this question is the destruction of the Flixborough chemical plant by an explosion, and the trade union involvement in the subsequent rebuilding of the site.

This is what Stan Davison, Assistant General Secretary ASTMS, had to say in a letter to Financial Times (19/6/75) following the enquiry into the disaster:

'The report rightly calls for the close involvement of the trade unions concerned. One of the ironies of the first 36 hours after the disaster was that management records and structures had totally disappeared and only the trade union representatives were able to provide much needed information, and generally cope with the situation. Despite this, the immediate investigations, that is police, company and local authority, made no reference to the trade union representatives for the first five days . . .

When the plant is rebuilt on this site, as it must be, it must incorporate the latest hardware, inspection and safety techniques; and it must involve the workpeople and their trade unions from day one.'

Of course, the problem is that workers are not always present from day one. In the Flixborough example, most workers were not taken on by the company until the original plant had been built. During the rebuilding of the works the great majority of the firm's employees were not present on the site. Does this create problems if workers are attempting to influence design decisions through trade union organisation and the extension of collective bargaining? Are there any other ways of developing workers' influence which could get round these problems, for example by having workers representatives on the board of companies?

A union representative on the board of the company might have been able to intervene in decisions affecting the safety of the plant before any workers were taken on at the new site. But of course some trade unionists have doubts about board representation. They are worried that unions can become too involved in management. This links to the questions raised in chapter 1 about the meaning of 'industrial democracy'. It shows that whenever trade unionists seek to extend their influence over new areas of management decision-making they face problems.

How should they extend their influence? Should they look for more joint involvement with management, or should they react to management's proposals only after these have been finalised?

How can workers exercise more influence over management planning without suffering an unacceptable loss of independence?

This chapter will not provide simple answers to these difficult questions. Later sections and programmes should help you examine the factors behind these dilemmas, and enable you to make up your mind about the issues.

Safety and health outside the workplace

Some trade unionists have claimed the right to influence not only the effects of the process of production inside the workplace, but also the impact of work on the community outside. Workers have put forward demands about the environmental effects of their work, and about the kind of products which the firms make.

Here is an extract from a wage claim put forward by unions in ICI in 1971 (the claim was called the 'Positive Employment Programme' — 'Pep')

'Our Environment

Pollution is the fashionable subject for discussion but it is not as a public relations exercise that we raise this matter as part of this claim. It is essential to the philosophy of 'Pep' that we as trade unionists share in making our company not only more prosperous but also more responsible. Here we address you not as 'management' but as fellow human beings who have to live together on this little planet called Earth.

Our members are anxious that the growth of their real incomes is not to be at the expense of the health of themselves, their families and their communities. We see this as a vital matter for trade unionists as trade unionists.

We ask that the terms of reference of the safety committees be extended to include the effects of the production process on the whole community, instead of just those who happen to be employed within ICI itself.

35

There is nothing idealistic about this — we are thinking of our members families and their children's children.'

Do you think that workers and trade unions have a right to comment on the social and environmental effects of the products they make?

Can you think of any environmental effects produced by your own firm or its products?

Should workers be able to refuse to make certain products?

Could workers effectively influence the product range of their company through the extension of collective bargaining?

Action Checklist on Health and Safety

● Obtain and study a copy of the Health and Safety Commission booklet 'Safety Representatives and Safety Committees', (HMSO). You may get it either from a government bookshop or perhaps through your union.

● Find out what your union policy is on the question of whether or not safety representatives functions should be performed by shop stewards.

● If you already have a safety committee at your workplace, use the materials in the chapter to discuss

a whether this committee is adequate

b how the structure and powers of this committee might be improved

● Use the materials in this chapter to discuss the development of union policy on the implementation of the Regulations on Safety Representatives and Safety Committees at your workplace. Issues to consider might be:

the functions of safety representatives

facilities for safety representatives

procedures for taking up safety grievances

the composition and powers of safety committees

information requirements

● Find out through your workplace representatives if management is currently planning any changes that might affect health and safety at work.

How much information is available to workplace representatives about management's plans?

How could these planned changes be improved from the workers point of view?

● Find out whether union representatives at your workplace have a small library of legislation, regulations, handbooks reports and booklets which may help trade unionists to deal with safety problems more effectively.

● Investigate union training opportunities for trade union safety representatives which are available in your locality. These might be 10 day courses for safety representatives, organised by the TUC, or shorter courses run by your union.

Is there an agreement in your workplace on paid release from work for safety representatives to attend courses?

● Obtain a copy of the 'Guidance Notes on Employers' Policy Statements for Health and Safety at Work'. This is available from your local Health and Safety Inspectorate. Obtain a copy of your employer's written statement on health and safety policy and compare this to the Guidance Notes. Does it meet all the points raised in the notes?

● Consider whether showing the TU Studies films 'Health and Safety' and 'Get organised — for safety's sake!' would aid fellow stewards, staff reps, or branch members in stimulating interest and debate about new policies on health and safety.

Chapter 3   Are You Happy In Your Work?

This chapter develops ideas and issues set out in Book 2 of Trade Union Studies — Trade Unions and the Economy, in the chapter 'New Jobs for Old'; and in Book 1 in the chapter 'Re-organisation at Work' (to obtain these see pp 183).

Questions

Note down your responses to these questions before watching the television programme or working through the chapter.

1 Consider your job and the job of the people you work along with, whether in manual or white-collar jobs:

Yes No
☐ ☐ Do they involve repeating fixed sets of tasks?

If yes, how long does the completion of each task take?
Seconds

Minutes

Hours

Do tasks have to be completed in a fixed time set by work study?

Yes No
☐ ☐ Are workers paced by machines?

To what extent does the job involve taking decisions and initiative?
☐ A great deal
☐ Very little
☐ Not at all

2 Who do you think has most influence on the nature of your job?
☐ You
☐ The machine designer
☐ The work study engineer
☐ The foreman

3 If you have experience of jobs being redesigned through the introduction of new methods of work or new machinery, did the changes make the jobs
☐ More satisfying
☐ Les satisfying
☐ No change

None	A Little	A Lot	
☐	☐	☐	**4** What sort of influence does your union have at present on Who does what jobs
☐	☐	☐	How work study is carried out
☐	☐	☐	The speed of assembly lines or machines

Is this the result of a formal agreement between unions and management, or just informal understandings with your supervisor?

5 Here are some typical remarks you will probably have heard from your members about work. Indicate whether you agree or disagree with these statements

Agree Disagree

☐ ☐ 'I don't care one way or the other about job satisfaction as long as the money is good'

☐ ☐ 'You spend a big part of your life at work so it ought to be satisfying'

☐ ☐ 'Factory work will always be boring and repetitive — that's the only way to make it efficient.'

☐ ☐ 'The best way to give workers more satisfaction would be to reduce the length of the working week.'

Yes No

☐ ☐ **6** Has job satisfaction ever been discussed as a union issue at your work place?

Issues for the chapter
After reading this chapter you should have a clearer understanding of:

● Why control over job design is an important part of the fight for industrial democracy.

● How jobs have changed since the industrial revolution.

● Why there has recently been a new interest among management in 'job satisfaction'.

● The problems for unions raised by various experiments in job satisfaction.

● What steps union representatives can take to raise job design as a bargaining issue.

Job satisfaction and industrial democracy
Your answers to the questionnaire will probably have shown that most workers have very little control over the nature of their jobs, and that most jobs are repetitive and boring.

The question we need to ask ourselves is: Can we honestly talk about industrial democracy in a situation where a small handful of people determine just what tasks the majority of workers will perform, day in, day out, and how these tasks will be carried out?

If unions are going to change this situation they need to get involved in the process of *job-design* — because it is job design that determines the way in which a particular production process or adminstrative process is broken down into separate jobs and tasks and how work is organised within these tasks. At present 'job design' is normally carried out by a small group of technical specialists.

We will see in this chapter that traditional methods of job design tend to take control from workers and give it to management. If we accept that industrial democracy is about increasing workers control over their working lives, then clearly we can't afford to ignore this area of job design.

A historical view:

The kinds of jobs we do today can be traced back to the Industrial Revolution and the beginnings of factory work:

'The Industrial Revolution brought about changes in methods of working, not only through the introduction of machines, but also by breaking down many jobs into a series of relatively simple tasks and increasing the specialisation of labour. The development of 'scientific management' principles, particularly by F. W. Taylor (1856-1917) accelerated this development. Taylor argued that not only were the operation of machines to be scientifically engineered, but that the operations of the worker should be planned with equal precision and should be determined with exactitude.'

Report of the Work of the Tripartite Group on Job Satisfaction, TUC Employment Policy Committee 1976.

It was when workers were brought together in factories that employers could for the first time exercise control over the way that work was done. When work was done at home, the only control employers had was on the amount of money paid for a particular piece of work. How much was produced, and how, was basically up to the workers. With the development of factories, management could extend their control over how people worked, when they took breaks, how the work was allocated between individuals, and how individuals performed the tasks allocated to them. In other words, many of those decisions which could previously be taken by the workers themselves passed into the hands of the new factory management.

As workers' jobs became more and more fragmented, the job of management or co-ordination became more and more important. At the same time, costs for management were reduced since fragmented tasks could be done by unorganised low paid unskilled labour.

In 1903 when the Ford Motor Company was founded, building automobiles was a task reserved for craftsmen. But as demand for Ford models increased, management needed to increase output, and to do this they needed more control over the production process. Special engineering talent was engaged to revise the production methods of the company. This led to the introduction of moving assembly lines, which probably had the biggest impact in doing away with craft skills and the job control that went with this. Control over the planning and organisation of work was transferred from the shop floor to management. Management now decided how work was divided up, the order in which tasks were done, the methods for doing each task, and the amount of time that this should take. The original Ford workers planned and organised work as well as carrying it out. The new style Ford workers were paid just to *do*, not to think and plan. They became just hired 'hands' and the brain work went to management.

In fact even before the First World War, F. W. Taylor, the father of scientific management and work study urged that 'all possible brain work should be removed from the shop floor and centred in the planning or laying-out department'.

*Ford Motor company's
factories pre 1914*

It is important to remember that the process of job design has had an effect
not just on individual jobs but on what can be called the 'authority structure'
of an organisation. The tendency has been to create a hierarchy or pyramid
of authority with more and more power to take decisions at the top and less
and less at the bottom.

Another important consequence of these changes is that specialisation is
increased not only between workers, but also between departments. One
department designs a product; another decides how the work involved in
making the product should be carried out; another department performs
the production work; another department checks that the product
conforms to the original design.

Typical early factory organisation

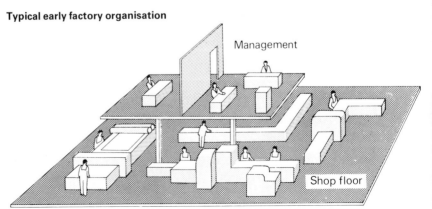

Management

Shop floor

Typical modern factory organisation

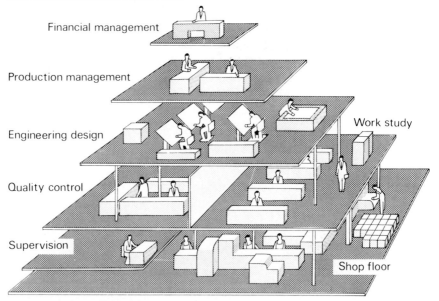

Financial management

Production management

Engineering design

Work study

Quality control

Supervision

Shop floor

Think about how the points made in the previous section relate to your workplace

Is there a department in your organisation that specialises in designing or measuring jobs?

Have you ever heard manual workers complain: 'I'd like a chance to use my brain as well as my hands'?

Or white collar workers say 'I'd like to do things with my hands more and not just deal with paperwork'?

Job design and efficiency:

Some people argue that the breaking down of jobs into simple operations is the only way to get efficiency. And a degree of specialisation in modern industry is undoubtedly essential. No one worker can be expected to master all the range of skills involved in producing a given product or service. But does specialisation always help efficiency? The more tasks are divided up, the greater the problems of co-ordination between departments and people. And all sorts of problems can arise when the people designing a job are different from the people actually doing the job. Something that looks fine on paper may not always work out in practice.

Can you think of examples in your organisation where this kind of specialisation causes problems?

This is what one report had to say about 'fragmented' jobs:

'Efficient' methods of production, such as rationalisation, specialisation, the subdivision of tasks, minimising skill requirements, may no longer work as effectively as they appear to do on the drawing board. People do not respond like machines.

43

. . . Frustration and resentment may be built up which can result in poor motivation, non-cooperation, poor quality work, absenteeism, high turnover and industrial unrest'.

'Make Work More Satisfying', Tripartite Steering Group on Job Satisfaction, Department of Employment 1975

🧍🧍🧍🧍 Does your organisation have problems of high absenteeism, high turnover, poor quality output?

Do you as a trade unionist, have information on this from management?

Is there any relation at your work place between levels of absenteeism, turnover, etc., and the kinds of jobs people are doing?

The new management interest in job design

A great deal of research has suggested that absenteeism, turnover and so on are at least partially related to the kind of work people do. And a number of employers have become sufficiently concerned about the effects of such problems on productivity that they have begun to rethink their approach to job design. This has been particularly true in Sweden, where both employers and trade unions have increasingly taken the view that both sides of industry can gain from a rethinking of job design based on a less mechanical approach to efficiency.

In 1972 the SAF (Swedish equivalent of the CBI) and the LO (Swedish equivalent of the TUC) signed an Agreement on Rationalisation which made this new approach clear:

'rationalisation shall seek to attain increased productivity, greater job satisfaction, a better working environment and security of employment. The job design activity must allow not only for technical and economic aspects, but also incorporate a conscious effort to create jobs that the individual can perceive to be meaningful and rewarding'.

Most important, the agreement stressed that workers must be fully involved in the process of job design and that —

'normal collective bargaining should be seen as the principal channel for the exercise of employee influence'.

In Sweden, therefore, job design is now very much on the agenda as a collective bargaining issue.

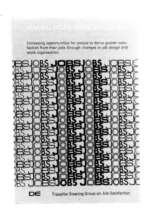

In the UK there has been no comparable *agreement* between the TUC and the CBI, but in 1973 a Tripartite Steering Group on Job Satisfaction was set up, whose members include representatives of Government, the TUC and CBI. On the group's recommendation, the Department of Employment has set up a Work Research Unit which carries out research projects and offers advice to employers and trade unions on job design. In 1975 the Steering Group published a report called 'Making Work More Satisfying' which emphasised in the same way as the Swedish agreement the benefits to employers and workers that could follow from a new approach to job design.

The report summarises the potential advantages to be gained from improved job design as follows:

Workers	Management & Workers	Management
1 More interesting work.	**1** Improved industrial Relations climate.	**1** Better quality.
2 Scope for development.	**2** Organisational growth.	**2** Reduced absence
3 More autonomy		**3** Lower turnover
4 Companionship and team pride.		**4** More flexibility
5 Share in any benefits to employers. (i.e. higher pay)		**5** Higher productivity.

The important question here is do management and workers gain *equally*? And are there any *losses* involved?

The following sections look at some experiments in job design and try to weigh up who benefits from the changes and how.

Experiments in job redesign

Experiments in job redesign are usually classified under the following headings — job rotation, job enlargement, job enrichment, and autonomous work groups. Some examples of each are set out below to help you make up your mind about how such experiments relate to union objectives.

Job rotation:

This is fairly self explanatory. The idea is to increase the variety in work by people rotating between jobs. This is usually done at regular intervals ranging from a few hours to several weeks, and is sometimes arranged on a less formal basis.

In fact the *design* of jobs is not changed, but each individual experiences a greater variety of tasks and might acquire new skills.

Job enlargement:

This involves amalgamating several tasks into a single job. Instead of repeatedly performing one operation on a product taking, say two minutes, a worker might perform three consecutive operations taking say six minutes — in other words, job cycles are lengthened. This can be achieved often without altering existing technology and so does not involve any extra capital expenditure for employers.

However, where job enlargement is extended to allow say one person to assemble a whole product, this does often mean changes in technology and machinery.

For example, at Philips Fan Heaters, Hamilton, assembly of fans was traditionally carried out on a flow line, using teams of from 6 to 14 semi-skilled workers who repeatedly performed one process on a flow of fans. In May 1966 opportunity was taken of the introduction of a new model to set up a special unit in which each operator would be responsible for the complete assembly of an appliance.

Job enrichment:

This means a worker takes on greater responsibility, e.g. by organising and checking his own work, or by being involved in decisions about planning and organising work normally taken by supervision. In other words, workers are given more chance to use their brains as well as their hands. The report 'Making Work More Satisfying' describes the following example from the Electricity Board accounts department:

The original situation

Work was split between offices, e.g. one office dealt with preparation of accounts, another with adjustment of those which were incorrect. There was further specialisation within these offices. Work was passed down from senior supervisor to section supervisor to junior supervisor to chargehand to clerks. When the decision to computerise the work was taken, the new system was designed in a way intended to produce satisfying jobs. This was some eight years ago.

The changes made

The 'unit clerk' system was adopted, whereby each clerk deals with all queries and all the work necessary to ensure that the customers in her care receive a correct account. Work flows directly to the unit clerk who refers to her supervisor only when she feels it necessary. Clerks liaise directly with those who arrange for work to be carried out on customers' premises. Supervisors now have more time for general supervision and training.

Autonomous work groups:

Again the division between 'thinking' and 'doing' is broken down, but this time on a group rather than just an individual basis. Groups of employees plan and organise work among themselves. The traditional role of supervisor tends to change to one of giving advice and support to the group.

The group has clear goals, such as producing a specified number of units per week, or completing a certain volume of work. But the means by which these targets are achieved are left very much to the group. This means that individuals within the group have some degree of choice as to whether they perform a large number of tasks or only a limited number. People may choose gradually to increase their range of skills over time.

Production groups may take on some of the functions previously left to specialist departments, such as quality control. Specialisation not only between individuals but also between departments can therefore be reduced.

Autonomous work groups can be established without making any alterations to existing technology, as an example from United Biscuits factory in Manchester shows:

The original situation

Production was, and still is, organised on flow lines, one line for each variety of biscuit produced. Workers on the lines were closely supervised and had no discretion as to how their jobs should be performed.

The changes made

Operators have been given authority to start up their lines and to shut them down if necessary. Now they can carry out simple maintenance, organise their own meal and other breaks, and work out job rotation or team work among themselves. They keep log books, and do paper work previously done by supervisors, and have weekly plant meetings with supervisors and plant management. In day-to-day working, management is only involved if the operators encounter a problem then cannot solve.

Some forms of autonomous group working on the other hand may involve a total rethinking of the technology and the organisation of production.

Probably the most famous example here is the one illustrated in detail in the TU studies film of the Volvo Kalmar plant in Sweden, where traditional assembly line methods of car production were totally abandoned and the new factory was specially designed for a new form of group assembly.

Here is how one journal described this experiment:

How they do it

(from the Economist 25 December, 1976)

Of the various techniques devised to "humanise" car production, Volvo's Kalmar plant (below) is the most striking. The straight, constantly-moving assembly line has been replaced by individual carriers, each loaded with a car body, travelling along a magnetic tape round a large circle. To give the impression of small secluded workshops, Volvo has dented the circle to fit it along the walls of a 12-cornered factory building.

The carrier passes through 28 assembly groups of 15 to 20 people at computer-controlled speeds varying from three metres per minute to 30 metres, depending on the difficulty of the job to be done. Each team has been assigned related operations, such as fitting the electrical equipment, to give them the impression that they are doing a "complete" job. At a few team stations, the carrier is shunted on to sidings for stationary operations, but most of the time the carrier continues moving.

People who want to see the body through all the jobs in their station can ride along on the carrier, which is about 65 cm high. Carriers can also be switched from computer to manual control, giving the workers some control over their speed. At the end of each station, there is provision for a "buffer" of two bodies. At the present throughput of 12.1 cars per hour, that means each team can have a 10-minute break. Workers rotate freely within teams, but there is little movement from one station to another. Cycles per team range from about 20 to 30 minutes, which means two to three minutes for each individual job. Small sub-assembly stations are dotted around the main line.

Keeping Volvo's workers calm at Kalmar

Section of the hexagonal beehive

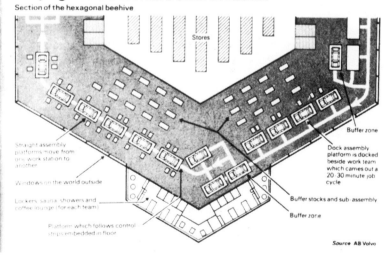

Stores

Straight assembly platforms move from one work station to another

Windows on the world outside

Lockers, sauna, showers and coffee lounge (for each team)

Platform which follows control strips embedded in floor

Buffer zone

Dock assembly platform is docked beside work team which carries out a 20-30 minute job cycle

Buffer stocks and sub-assembly

Buffer zone

Source AB Volvo

47

Who benefits and how
The Management side

In all the experiments described above the initiative came from management because they were experiencing particular problems with absenteeism, turnover, low productivity or high defects. So did the changes solve their problems?

Certainly there was some improvement in all cases, even if not always as great as expected.

At Philips there was a 50% reduction in defects, and output increased by 10%.

At the Electricity Board, 'output per clerk has consistently exceeded the norm that was expected when the new system was planned'.

At United Biscuits there were improvements in labour turnover and absenteeism, although no marked increase in productivity.

At Volvo's Kalmar plant, absenteeism and turnover, which had been as high as 20% and 100% in a year respectively at traditional Volvo assembly plants, were reduced but not as much as Volvo hoped. The rate of assembling cars at Kalmar is about the same as at other Volvo plants.

It is worth noting that the cost savings at Kalmar have not been great enough to offset the company's 10% extra investment cost of abandoning the traditional assembly line.

(As reported in The Financial Times 23/11/76)

This raises the question of how far management will be prepared (or should be expected) to make improvements in job design when there is no financial 'return' in it for them.

Management gains/Union problems

1 In all schemes, management is likely to get a greater flexibility and interchangeability of labour. This might give workers access to greater skills and variety, but it can cause problems in terms of craft and skill demarcations and differentials.

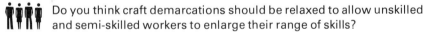 **Do you think craft demarcations should be relaxed to allow unskilled and semi-skilled workers to enlarge their range of skills?**

What arguments would you put forward if you were a craft worker?

What arguments would you put forward if you were an unskilled worker?

2 More flexible working is likely to reduce management's overall demand for labour which might mean redundancies. With job enrichment and autonomous groups, the jobs of supervisors and 'indirect' workers are likely to be affected also.

3 Management may also be able to cut labour costs by getting workers to take on new skills and responsibilities 'on the cheap'. Most agreements provide for pay increases so that workers get a share of cost savings. But it is not always easy to predict in advance what these savings will be.

4 Management may see autonomous work groups as a way of undermining collective solidarity and union organisation. A report of the Volvo experiment by the LO and SAF says that union leaders are thinking about pressing to have work group representatives chosen through trade union machinery, which does not happen at present, in order to ensure firm links with the wider union organisation.

'The Volvo Kalmar Plant: The Impact of New Design on Work Organisation', The Rationalisation Council, SAF/LO

The worker side
Clearly the benefits to workers will vary widely from scheme to scheme but we can make some general points.

Job rotation and job enlargement

Job rotation and less ambitious forms of job enlargement are likely to have least impact. A worker merely performs two or three fragmented jobs instead of one. And three boring jobs can be just as boring as one.

With job rotation and job enlargement, the balance of benefits is likely to be in management's favour. Job content is still very much defined by management and there are no real changes in the authority and decision making structure. Changes tend to take place *within* existing technology, which must limit their impact.

Job enrichment and autonomous work groups
Job enrichment and autonomous work groups offer more opportunity for a genuine increase in the skill, and decision making content of workers jobs. In autonomous work groups, workers can very often determine their own job content, as well as taking on supervisory functions of planning and control.

Some control can be taken back from management to the shop floor. But these new forms of work organisation also raise problems for unions:

Pay Autonomous work groups tend to encourage group bonus systems, which can put a lot of group pressure on older and less adaptable workers.

Skill demarcation We have raised this point already and this is something unions would need to look at carefully.

Taking on management responsibility Autonomous work group take on responsibility for meeting certain targets — but these are targets set by management.

A trade union objective could be to make the group targets the subject of negotiation.

One attraction for management of autonomous work groups is that discipline and supervision tend to become more self-imposed by the group. This links back to the question we raised in chapter 1 of the extent to which workers should take on responsibility for matters like production performance.

 How would you tackle these problems if you were involved in an autonomous work group experiment?

A new role for supervisors?
We have seen that in some kinds of job redesign workers organise and supervise their own work. So what about the supervisor? Does he become redundant?

In Sweden where experiments with autonomous work groups have been widespread the unions have had to agree a policy on the role of supervisors.

The Swedish unions' view is that the role of the supervisor should remain but could become a very different one.

'He may have to give greater attention to the relations existing between his own department and the rest of the firm, so as to create optimum conditions for the effective functioning of the various more or less autonomous groups'.

'Industrial Democracy', Programme adopted by the 1971 Congress of Swedish Trade Union Confederation, LO.

In Sweden it would seem that the supervisors' unions have in fact welcomed the idea of a change in their role to one of support and joint co-operation rather than authority.

In 1974 the Swedish Confederation of Supervisory Employees and the Metal Workers' Union published this joint statement:

'. . . the Confederation of Supervisory Employees and the Metalworkers' Union believe they have a joint responsibility to work for changes in company organisation in the direction of a decentralisation of decisions. We believe that it is urgent that groups of employees, together with supervisors, be granted greater authority and responsibility so that they can jointly plan, organise and check their own production work.'

Quoted in 'Job Reform in Sweden', SAF

Are supervisors in your firm unionised?

Are supervisors in the same union as other workers?

Do you think workers should be interested in the problems of supervisors?

Can you think of reasons from your own experience why supervisors might be frustrated with their present position and welcome a change in their role?

Here are some questions to help you think about this —

● Are supervisors resented by workers as authority figures and representatives of management?

● Are supervisors 'by passed' by shop stewards and management in communications and dealing with grievances?

● Is there a tendency for more and more decisions to be taken away from supervisors and transferred to specialist levels higher up the organisation? Do you think autonomous work groups would help any of these problems?

Job satisfaction and Union priorities
There are a number of different union attitudes to questions of job satisfaction and job enrichment. The following quotations illustrate some of the different approaches. Bearing in mind some of the issues raised in this chapter, think over which of the statements you agree with or disagree with.

'The manipulative aspect of . . . management approaches . . . can readily be seen in the case of job enrichment. Job enrichment is introduced by

management in order to complement or to replace other methods for securing managerial objectives'.

'Industrial Democracy' TUC

'The United Auto Workers of the USA have not yet been convinced of the validity of experiments at Volvo and Saab and is giving priority to seeking a substantial reduction in the length of the working week, and also a retirement age of 40 for motor assembly workers'.

Quoted in 'Job Satisfaction', ed. Mary Weir, Fontana

'Job satisfaction for unions would seem to assume a very low priority with so many people without jobs at all'.

TUC

'British unions should not . . . tolerate job enrichment being advanced separately, either as a bargaining subject or as an innovatory management practice . . . There is a clear need to bargain about the *whole sequence* of managerial decisions which really control job content, security and prospects. These start with the prior planning . . . of new investment programmes'.

also in 'Job Satisfaction', ed. Mary Weir

Workers at the Meriden Co-operative

It might be argued that full 'job satisfaction' can only be achieved where workers have control not only over their own jobs but over all aspects of the management decision-making process — in other words where there is workers' self-management. This is the view taken by one commentator on the Meriden motor-cycle co-operative:

'One of the first things they decided was that supervisors and foremen would be a superfluous and irritating anomaly and that they would not employ anybody for this function but would have organisers and co-ordinators only, appointed by the shop steward directors. Job enlargement and rotation have become quite commonplace and flexibility of labour (all workers are paid a flat rate of £50 per week) means that bottle necks can be overcome quickly. These achievements are the envy of many employers who have taken a close interest in Meriden for this very reason, wondering whether they can replicate this situation in their own factories. Unfortunately for them, this happy state of affairs can only be achieved where employers are abolished and men and women are convinced they are 'working for themselves' as are the Meriden workers'.

'The New Worker Co-operatives', K Coates ed, Spokesman Books.

Job design as a collective bargaining issue

In 1970 unions and management at ICI agreed on a programme of job enlargement and job enrichment as part of the Weekly Staff Agreement. The agreement contained a no-redundancy pledge.

A year's experience made it very clear to the unions that work organisation could not be separated from wider issues such as disclosure of information, manpower planning and investment.

Here are some of the points the unions made in their 1971 claim to management.

They expressed concern that the 'no-redundancy pledge' was being met by restrictions on recruitment, particularly of young workers, and called for 'a joint review of manpower requirements'. Linked to this concern for maintaining as well as improving jobs, they also demanded joint discussions on investment programmes.

As regards the monitoring of the job enrichment programme, the unions made it clear that 'If there is to be long-run confidence in the operation of the system, it will be necessary to establish *mutuality* in access to and analysis of the relevant control and cost data'.

From the trade union point of view, therefore, job satisfaction and job enrichment may not be, as some managements tend to imply, 'separate' shop floor questions. They can then only really be dealt with as part of a whole process of extending the range of collective bargaining to cover all aspects of management decision-making.

The link between investment decisions and job design is particularly important. It is when new plant and machinery are being installed that the opportunities for changes in work organisation are greatest. Often there is little that can be done to radically change jobs within the confines of existing plant and technology.
As the TUC have pointed out —

'At present', investment decisions are made far too often with only the increases that can be made in efficiency in mind . . . Decisions on new plant will broadly determine working methods for the life of that investment, which in the case of some heavy machinery can extend to 30 or 40 years'.

Report on the Work of the Tripartite Group on Job Satisfaction, TUC.

In the film programme, British Leyland stewards reported on their own trip to Sweden to examine the Volvo ideas in action.

Unions in British Leyland are discussing questions of job design as part of the wider extension of joint decision-making within the firm following the Ryder Report. Two major new investment programmes here relate to the building of a new Rover factory and to the launching of the new Mini model.

In the case of the new Mini, the Car Council, one of the joint management committees set up as part of Leyland's new participation structure, decided to set up a special sub-committee to examine the alternative methods by which the new model could be manufactured. A union representative has commented:

'Instead of waiting for the planning committee — composed of the professional specialists on machinery, production techniques, and methods of work — to finalise their proposals, we decided to sit down with them and work out the alternatives'.

(From a report in The Financial Times 15/10/76.)

Of course, union influence on improving the working life of their members need not be restricted to occasions of major new investment. There are a number of much more immediate ways in which unions can increase the control exercised by workers over their work experience.

An important starting point, if you do not have this provision already, is the negotiation of a 'status quo' agreement, which states that management cannot make any changes in work organisation, the allocation of work, the speed of machines or assembly lines without first discussing the matter with the union.

We looked briefly at this in Chapter 1 and it is discussed more fully in the chapter on 'Reorganisation of Work' in the Year 1 Book of Trade Union Studies.

Another matter that should be made the subject of joint agreement where relevant is the operation of work study techniques. As we have seen, the application of such techniques can have a profound effect on the nature of a workers job, and work study should only be carried out within a framework of agreed rules.

Where groups of workers are particularly frustrated with their present jobs, unions can put to management their own proposals for job enrichment or autonomous work groups.

Action checklist

● Decide if your dispute procedure should contain a 'status quo' clause to enable proper negotiations on new working practices and methods.

● Decide whether you should have an agreement on the application of work study techniques where this is relevant.

● Ask management for regular information on absenteeism, turnover, output, quality and defects on a workplace and departmental basis.

● Look carefully at this information to see if it points to any areas of high membership frustration with their work. If it does, discuss with the membership how work organisation could be improved.

● Ask management for information on their future investment plans on new products, new plants, etc.

● Discuss the question of job satisfaction and job design at your branch.

Consider whether showing the TU studies film 'Are you happy at your work?' would stimulate interest and debate (to obtain it, see pp 183).

Checklist for negotiations on job redesign

If you decide to raise the issue in negotiations with management, here are some points to keep in mind:

● Adequate financial reward for increased skills, responsibility, relaxation of demarcations.

● Agreement that workers will share in future financial benefits.

● Full disclosure of all information necessary to assess these benefits and monitor the progress of the project.

● Safeguards against redundancy and job loss through natural wastage.

● Joint monitoring of future manpower requirements.

● Full involvement of all unions whose members will be affected directly or indirectly by the scheme.

● Consultants on job design to be accountable to the unions as well as management, with full union access to the relevant documents and information.

Further reading

'Making Work More Satisfying' Tripartite Steering Group on Job Satisfaction, HMSO 1975.
'Labor and Monopoly Capital' Harry Braverman, Monthly Review Press, 1974.
'Job Satisfaction' edited by Mary Weir, Fontana.
'An Outline of Work Study and Payment by Results' TUC 1970.
'Reorganisation at Work', Year 1 Trade Union Studies Book, BBC Publications 1975. (See pp 183).
'New Jobs for Old', Year 2 Trade Union Studies Book, BBC Publications 1975. (See pp 183).

Chapter 4   Sisters and Brothers

This chapter is about women at work. It would be valuable to remind
yourself of the chapter in Book 1 of Trade Union Studies which dealt in
detail with issues of equal pay for women and examined how attitudes to
women at work can affect union workplace policy on pay. This chapter
follows on from that to ask how women's rights at work link in to the wider
issues of industrial democracy which we have been looking at.

General questions

Note down your answers to the following questions before watching the television programme or working through the chapter.

PART I **Women in your union**

1 How many women employees at your workplace are union members?
Part-time women . . . .
Full-time women . . . .

2 How many women shop stewards are there?

3 How many women on average attend:
workship union meetings? . . . .
branch meetings? . . . .

4 Have you ever discussed issues of equal pay or sex discrimination at your workplace or branch meetings? . . . .

PART II **Women at work**

1 How many women are employed at your workplace? . . . .
2 How many of these women work part-time? . . . .
3 What are the average weekly earnings of women? . . . .
What are the average weekly earnings of men? . . . .
4 What are the main jobs that women do? . . . .
Do men also do these jobs? . . . .
. . . .
. . . .

5 How many men and women get training in your company—

	Men	Women
Apprentice		
Day-Release		
Sandwich Course		
In-Company		

In previous chapters, two main points have been emphasised:
1 You can't have industrial democracy without strong trade union organisation that is fully representative of the membership and accountable to the membership.

2 Strong union organisation gives workers the power to extend their rights at work and bring more decisions under joint control.
It follows that if any particular group of workers is weakly organised and discriminated against by management, then this weakens the position of all workers. That is why women's rights, like immigrant workers' rights — are a key issue for all active trade unionists. Your answers to Part I of the questionnaire will probably have shown that women are not very well organised and are less involved in union matters than men. That is why this chapter starts by looking at women in unions before going on to look at some of the key areas for women's rights.

Issues for the chapter

After reading through this chapter you should have a clearer idea of —

1 The problems women face becoming active in the union.

2 What unions can do to get round these problems.

3 How you can tackle inequality at your workplace through negotiations.

PART I **Women in Unions**

While women are still not as strongly unionised as men, the proportion of women members in unions has been slowly growing, so that while in 1930 only about 1 in 8 TUC members were women, by 1975 this figure had risen to 1 in 4.

In particular unions women account for a very high percentage of total union membership. In traditional 'womens industries' this has long been the case; for example in the Tailor and Garment Workers Union and the National Union of Hosiery and Knitwear Workers, women account for about three quarters of the total membership. The same is true in the National Union of Teachers. But more recently there has also been a rapid expansion of women membership in the general and public service unions:

For example, in NUPE the percentage of women members has risen from 24% in 1950 to 62% in 1974.

In COHSE the percentage of women members rose from 38% in 1950 to 67% in 1974.

The expansion in public service unions is mainly due to rising membership among women. And it is this expansion that has helped keep up overall trade union membership in this country, as traditional industries have declined.

The important issue for all trade unionists is how to make sure that this growing number of women members are *active* members.

 What proportion of the members in your union are women? How has this figure changed over time?

Turning 'cardholders' into activists

Look at the questions at the beginning of the chapter. How many women attended union meetings? How many women were shop stewards?
It is a common complaint that you can't get women to meetings. Those unions that have tried to collect figures on the number of women shop stewards or branch officers have usually found that women take up much less than their share of places.
This is what a NUPE survey showed:

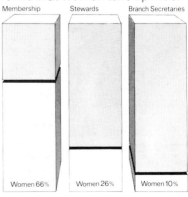

Membership — Women 66%
Stewards — Women 26%
Branch Secretaries — Women 10%

This is also true higher up in the unions. If you look at table 1 you will see how poorly women are represented on national executives and among full-time officials, even in unions that have a very high proportion of women members.

 Is your union on this table?

TABLE 1 Women in Unions 1974

Union	No. of women members	women as % total membership	National Executive		Full-time Officials	
			men	women	men	women
NUPE	294,640	62.6	—	—	136	—
GMWU	269,263	31.2	—	—	136	4
TGWU	266,348	14.9	—	—	500	4
NALGO	200,503	38.7	52	8	—	6
NUT	186,146	74.3	35	7	12	2
USDAW	184,248	56.4	16	1	124	5
AUEW (Eng)	154,169	13.1	—	—	—	1
CPSA	147,549	68.4	20	6	12	3
NUTGW	101,190	86.5	11	4	41	7
COHSE	80,722	66.6	27	1	35	1
APEX	68,678	53.9	—	4	49	1
SOGAT	68,284	36.4	—	—	—	—
EEPTU	54,443	12.9	14	—	170	—
NUHKW	52,183	72.7	—	—	—	—
UPW	48,602	25.0	14	5	11	1
ASTMS	45,100	14.5	—	—	22	4
Bakers Union	22,804	43.1	15	3	23	1
NU Dyers & Bleachers	21,433	38.8	—	—	—	—
Ceramic & ATU	20,436	52.8	20	2	—	—
Tobacco Workers Union	13,726	65.6	13	3	6	3
NUBE		48.0	7	1	14	3

Figures from Organising Women Workers, Judith Hunt. WEA Studies for Trade Unionists.

Of the 37 members of the TUC General Council, only 2 are women and these are specially reserved seats — a question we will return to later.

How can unions change this?
Clearly the only way to get better representation of women at all levels of the union is to start at grass roots level.
Why is it that women's involvement in work place and branch union activity is often low?

● Is it because women aren't interested in union issues?

● Or is it because unions don't always organise their affairs in such a way as to encourage women's involvement?

Here are some questions that will help you think about this.

👥👥 Think about your union organisation —
How often are workplace and branch meetings held after work when women have children to look after?

How much work do shop stewards have to do out of working time, which could again clash with women's home responsibilities?

How often are union training schools held at weekends when women couldn't possibly attend unless someone else would look after the children?

Many women have problems becoming active in the union because they have *two* jobs — as workers during the day and as wives and mothers in the evenings and at weekends.

👥👥 Have you ever had discussions at your workplace as to how you might overcome some of these problems?

Has your union put forward any recommendations for overcoming these kinds of problems?

Some unions have conducted special surveys on the position of women both at work and within the union and here are some of the suggestions they have come up with on this particular point:

Meeting in working time
The GMWU stress that 'A great help to working mothers would be given by shop stewards negotiating with management where it does not already exist the right to hold workplace meetings *during working time* with no loss of pay.' A NALGO Equal Rights Working Party also urged that branch meetings should be held during working time where there were workplace branches.

Time-off with pay for union representatives to carry out their duties
This may be common practice already in many workplaces — but it is by no means universal. NALGO have stressed that formal agreements with management on this isuue would do a lot to encourage women to take on union office. Often where informal understanding exist, some new women shop stewards may not be aware of this — and management may take advantage of this to restrict their union activity.

Creche facilities at all meetings outside working-time
This might sound a formidable task, but it is worth thinking about and can really make a big difference for women with children. All it requires is the hiring of an extra room and the drawing up of a rota of people willing to staff the creche or playgroup — perhaps from among the husbands of women members in the branch!

(And of course the provision of creche facilities should apply to *all* union meetings. How many union conferences passing motions on equal opportunity for women think of providing creche factilities which would enable *women* to attend as delegates?)

PATTERNS OF DISCRIMINATION
AGAINST WOMEN
IN THE FILM & TELEVISION
INDUSTRIES

Special sub-committees at branch and workplace level
An ACTT study 'Patterns of Discrimination' recommended the setting up of special sub-committees to investigate and discuss the position of women in particular companies.

These committees could make sure that union policy on women was being carried out, and could discuss ways of drawing more women into union activity. The NALGO Equal Rights Report also stressed the need 'for meetings specifically to discuss issues affecting women particularly at branch and district level.' The work of such meetings and sub-committees can be an important way of attracting women into union activities and demonstrating to them that the union is concerned about their problems. Most important, through working in special sub committees, women with no previous experience of union activity may gain confidence in their own abilities to organise and do union work.

Taking women's needs into account when planning union training

If your branch or division holds weekend schools, then creche facilities are really vital if most women members are not to be automatically excluded. Many women may be reluctant to become or to remain shop stewards because they lack experience, and union training courses take place at awkward times. Residential courses are usually impossible for women unless they have husbands prepared to look after themselves *and* the children. And even day-release courses may cause problems for women who like to get away in time to meet the children from school.

In 1976 NUPE's London division experimented with a pilot scheme for shop steward training for women, which lasted half a day every week for twenty weeks.

Putting your own house in order

Even if all unions were to make these kinds of provisions real progress would still depend a lot on the attitudes of individual trade unionists.

 Have you ever heard a fellow trade unionist complain about women not being active in the union, and then the next day grumble that he had a cold dinner last night, or had to look after the children and miss football, because his wife was out on union business?

As the GMWU Guide to Negotiators emphasises —

'Men can do much to encourage the active participation of women in trade unions. As husbands they can encourage their wives to join; and they can accept their share of family responsibilities so that women are able to attend branch meetings, union conferences and participate in educational programmes.'

The TU Studies film 'Equal Pay' with the extracts from the Red Ladder play, provides an amusing stimulus for discussion of these questions of attitude for committees and branches (to obtain it, see pp 183).

Positive discrimination in unions

It has been argued that in order to break through the vicious circle of under-representation we have been looking at, 'positive discrimination' in favour of women may be necessary.

'But isn't it now illegal to discriminate in any way between men and women'? you may be asking.

In fact the Sex Discrimination Act does recognise that certain kinds of positive discrimination may be necessary if women are to 'catch up' and really achieve equality. This means that trade unions can within the new law

— reserve a minimum number of seats for women on elected bodies
— hold single-sex training courses (like the NUPE course we looked at earlier).

Special provisions for women within unions are not new: they can take the form of reserved seats for women on committees, women's conferences, or special women's committees.

Since 1931 there has been a Women's TUC and a TUC National Women's Advisory Committee and 2 seats on the General Council specially reserved for women.

Since 1938 the TUC has had a women officer.

Individual unions having National Women's Officers or Organisers are GMWU, TGWU, AUEW/TASS, and COHSE, and the GMWU and the AUEW Engineering Section also have separate Women's Conferences. Some individual unions also follow the general Council example of making special provision for women on their executives; the Tobacco Workers Union reserves two seats on its executive for women, the TSSA one seat and AUEW/TASS one seat for a representative of the National Women's Sub-Committee.

The question being debated within many unions now is whether such special provisions need to be extended to make women fully active in union affairs; or whether the continuation of such special provisions in fact holds back progress with 'token' gestures and by separating off women activists in special committees and conferences.

Reserved seats for Women
The TUC 1976 conference had two motions on this issue — one calling for an increase in the number of reserved seats for women on the General Council, and one calling that this special provision be ceased altogether. In 1975 a NUPE special conference on union reorganisation voted to reserve 5 seats on the executive for women, but the NALGO Equal Rights Working Party concluded that 'the creation of token women's places would be a set-back for the promotion of equal rights'.

Lets look at some arguments for and against reserved seats:

AGAINST ... unless women are brought up to think they are equal, and to act equal, and thereby play an active part within their trade union as trade unionists in the same way as their male colleagues, the Sex Discrimination Act will not serve its real purpose and will be defeated. We should not on the one hand demand that there be no discrimination against women and then immediately ask that women should be given preferential treatment.' *(Ms V McQuaid TSSA, 1976 TUC)*

FOR 'I can appreciate and understand the feeling this is discrimination in favour of women, but at the end of the day I feel that if we do not discriminate positively, in five, ten, fifteen or twenty years time we will still be hearing platitudes from this rostrum about "let the women have an equal chance and fight with the men". I would predict that within a very short time when the women who are elected on the Executive on this basis

have demonstrated beyond any shadow of doubt that they are capable of doing the job, they will increasingly stand for the general seats; and after a period of time it may be possible to then abolish the special seats for women one by one'.
(Bernard Dix, NUPE Special National Conference on Union Reorganisation)

What are your views on these arguments?

Can you see any function for special reserved seats for women within your local union organisation?

Special Women's Conferences

The debate over the need for separate women's organisations — from the caucus in the local branch to the Women's TUC — has been going on for several years in many unions.

The arguments for and against the Women's TUC have been summarised in the ACTT report 'Patterns of discrimination':

AGAINST 'Basically those opposed to separate organisation say that it means women's issues are "hived off" from the main TUC; and that women who might go to the TUC proper are "hived off" into the less important and powerless women's TUC. As a result the Women's TUC institutionalises the secondary importance of both women members and women's issues, rather than overcoming it.'

As a speaker at the TUC 1975 Women's Conference said 'We do believe that its continued existence inhibits full participation in the TUC, because it is so easy for a paternal attitude to be adopted towards us and to be told to take our problems to the appropriate place. Its like saying to a child "Mother is too busy, go and play in the corner".'

IN FAVOUR 'Those in favour say not only would abolition not be a guarantee of increased representation of women at the TUC; it could also mean that there would be even less discussion of women's needs than is possible now through the Women's TUC. And only in the Women's TUC can women trade unionists gain the necessary experience and confidence — as well as a hearing — to enable them to push effectively for their demands.'

The Women's Advisory Committee in their report to the 1970 TUC Women's Conference said they would welcome the time when it was no longer necessary to hold the conference, but they did not believe that time had yet arrived.

The arguments are much the same at whatever level of the union structure the need for separate womens meetings is discussed.

In the light of these arguments, what would your response be if it was proposed at your branch to set up a separate women's section or caucus in order to get women more involved?

Special sub-committees on women and equal rights

The reports by both NALGO and ACTT, while opposed to special women's conferences, argued strongly in favour of special national committees responsible for co-ordinating action against discrimination. Among the functions recommended for the ACTT Committee on Equality are compiling information on the position of women, formulating recommendations and policies for members and the union to push for, analysing changes in the law, and conducting propaganda campaigns.

After pressure from women members, including picketing of NEC meetings, ASTMS has established in 1975 a similar national committee with elected representatives from all divisions. Muriel Turner, the Assistant General Secretary had argued strongly against the development:

'I take the view very strongly that if you separate, or form a women's committee, then the executive when it's confronted with a women's issue will just say "Oh, refer it to the women's committee" rather than saying it's our problem, let's press the Minister on it or whatever.'
(Quoted in Women at Work, Lindsay Mackie and Polly Pattullo, Tavistock, 1977)

Members in favour of the committee argued that although the union had a fine 'Programme for Women Members', there would be no way of knowing just what progress was being made in implementing this policy unless there was a committee with special responsibility for monitoring developments and publicising the programme.

In most ASTMS divisions special Action Committees against Sex Discrimination have also been set up, again with the aim of compiling information on the position of women, formulating recommendations for members to act on, monitoring progress, and holding meetings and talks.

 Do you see a role for special committees of this nature at any level in your union?

The case for union solidarity
Some of you, both men and women, may be thinking, 'is all this special effort really worth it; the majority of women just don't want to be involved in unions; their families come first, they work for pin money and company, and so you can't expect them to get seriously involved in trade unions, or for unions to take their problems as seriously as mens.'
Let's look more carefully at some of the issues raised here. You might find yourself having to answer these kinds of arguments at union meetings, if you start pushing for priority treatment for women's rights.

'Women only work for pin money — work isn't as important to them as it is to the male breadwinner'

This kind of argument tends to imply that women are a very marginal part of the workforce. But 39% of the working population are women. Two-thirds of all working women work full-time, many of them combining jobs with looking after a family.

As NALGO points out: 'Women, like men, work because they need to *survive* — not just for 'extras'. The last major household survey revealed that just over 1 in 5 households were *solely* dependent on women's earnings. Other households depend on women's earnings to keep above the poverty line.

The DHSS has estimated that the number of two-parent families living in poverty in which the father was already in full-time work would have trebled if the father's income had not been supplemented by that of a working wife.

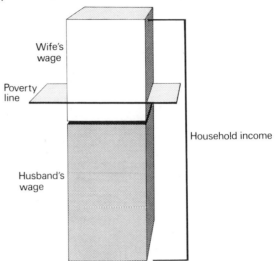

The rate for the job

The trade union principle is the rate for the job regardless of whether a person is single or married, childless or with a family. It is the job that is assessed, not the person. When did a negotiator ever argue that a man with two children should get more money than a man with none? The tax system is meant to take care of that. So whether or not women have dependents should have no influence at all on whether or not Unions are willing to back women fully in their struggle for equal pay.

'Women aren't prepared to fight for their rights'

You often hear the complaint that 'women don't support the men in their struggles. — You don't see them on the picket lines. And they won't even fight for their own rights — they seem happy to let management walk all over them. So why should men bother?'

It is true that some women are worried that if they fight for equal pay they will lose their jobs. Because that is what management and some male trade unionists are always telling them — that really equal pay wouldn't be in their interests. Employers used to intimidate workers like this in the 19th century — wage demands would mean unemployment; but workers refused to accept this false 'choice' and found that it is usually possible to use union organisation to fight for jobs *and* decent pay. This is what male trade unionists should be telling women — not that equal pay wouldn't help them.

When it comes to striking, women again have special problems — who looks after the children while mum is on the picket line? But in spite of the difficulties, women have shown on lots of occasions that they can hold out as well in strikes as anyone else. More and more women are realising that this is often the only way to get their rights fully established in practice. And it is not only women who at times show a lack of trade union solidarity:

● how many examples have you come across of men crossing picket lines on equal pay strikes?

● how often do male trade unionists agree with management that women should go first in redundancy situations (blatantly endorsing the 'pin money' argument)

● can men expect support from women in their struggles if they don't support women in theirs?

History has shown repeatedly that the existence of badly organised low-paid labour is a real threat to the living standards of all workers. It gives the employer the opportunity, often through mechanisation, of substituting cheap unskilled labour for skilled, well-organised and 'expensive' labour. It was precisely this realisation that lay behind the efforts of skilled workers at the end of the last century to organise unskilled workers. All too often these lessons aren't applied to the position of women.

How would you explain to a male member of your branch that it was in their interests to actively campaign for women's rights and strong trade union organisation among women?

How would you explain to women members of your branch that it was in their interests and the interests of all workers to be strongly organised and to fight for their rights?

PART II **Negotiating for Women's Rights**

Look back at your answers to Part II of the questionnaire at the beginning of the chapter; this should give you an idea of some of the problems of equal rights at your work place.

The best way to convince all women of the value of union organisation and activity is to get discussions going in your workplace about what women's problems are and how they can be improved through negotiations. No negotiator can afford to think that women's problems are being solved through the operation of the Equal Pay Act and the Sex Discrimination Act. The chapter in the Year 1 book looked in detail at what the Equal Pay Act means, and of course it is important that negotiators make sure that employers are at least complying with the terms of the Act.

But the problem of relying on the law was clearly shown by the Electrolux case in 1977. This showed that although one woman in a grade might win an equal pay case this means nothing for the other women in the grade, unless management can be forced through negotiation to make the individual remedy a collective one. Even more important, for a large number of women the Equal Pay Act is irrelevant. They work in 'female ghettos' where there are no men to claim 'equal pay' with.

There is overwhelming evidence that even where management have long accepted the principle of equal pay, women are by no means equal with men. For example, the NALGO Equal Rights Working Party reports that 'The principle of equal pay has been established in NALGO services for many years'. But a survey of members earnings showed clearly that women still lagged far behind in terms of pay. For example, while only 8% of men fell below the TUC low pay target of £30, 35% of women fell below this figure. The reasons for this become fairly clear when you look at how men and women are distributed between grades.

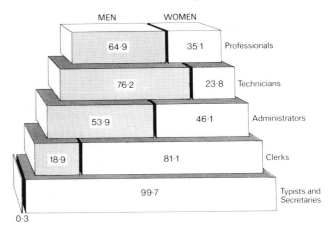

You can see that the bottom two grades of job are almost exclusively 'women's grades'.

How does this compare with the situation at your work place? Look back at your answers to the questions at the beginning of the chapter.

What we are concerned with in the rest of this chapter is why, even with technical 'equal pay', women still do not enjoy full equality, and what negotiators can do about this.

Women's Handicaps

There are a number of reasons why women remain trapped in low-pay, low-skill jobs:

● lack of training on entering employment — employers tend to argue it is not worth training women because they leave to have families.

● the fact that many women break their employment to have a family often puts paid to any real promotion prospects. In the past they have often had to restart at the bottom of the ladder.

● family responsibilities and lack of child-care provisions mean that many women have to work part-time. (30% of all women workers work less than 30 hours a week) Most part-time work is badly paid and restricted to lower skilled jobs. Many women have to give up work during the school holidays and can therefore only do temporary work.

● women with skills and training can be out of touch and 'rusty' after a break for a family, and without adequate retraining or 'refresher' courses may be forced back into less skilled work.

● many employers are simply prejudiced against women. A Government survey on 'Management Attitudes and Practices Towards Women at Work' found that even where a woman has the same or better qualifications than a man, many managers just prefer a man.

Negotiating maternity leave

We have seen that many of the disadvantages of women at work stem from the fact that they break their work to have children. We now have legislation in the form of the maternity leave provisions of the Employment Protection Act which at least acknowledges this problem and does something to tackle it. Under the Act

● a woman has the right to be re-instated in her job for up to 29 weeks after the birth of the baby.

● a woman has a right to six weeks maternity pay at 90% of a basic week's pay minus the state maternity allowance.

● dismissal of a woman purely or mainly on grounds of pregnancy is unfair dismissal.

How could you improve these rights?

Trade unionists should always aim to improve on legal minima in negotiated agreements. So where do these maternity leave provisions need improving?

2 year qualification period

A woman has to have worked somewhere for two years before she is eligible for maternity leave under the Act. This can effectively exclude large numbers of women who may have to change jobs frequently because of existing family responsibilities, or because their husband is moving jobs.

Part-timers excluded

The provisions do not apply to women working for less than 16 hours a week, or 8 hours a week if they have worked for their employer for five years. This once more excludes a large number of women.

Periods of leave compare unfavourably with other countries legal provisions

Let's look at what women in some European countries enjoy by right:

Austria	1 year paid maternity leave.
France	14 weeks leave at 90% of basic wage.
Hungary	5 months leave on full pay. 3 years leave with monthly cash allowances. Full reinstatement rights.
Italy	20 weeks leave on 80% of basic wage.
Sweden	Leave for *either parent* after the birth, with cash benefits payable on equal terms to either mother or father.

The period of 29 weeks after confinement within which a woman can return to the same or similar job under the Employment Protection Act may be far too short to give many women opportunity to make adequate child care provisions. If a woman can't find a nursery place in time and has to take more time off, she loses all her legal rights to reinstatement and may be back again at the bottom of the ladder!

No provision for full continuity of employment

Up to now women have had to pay for having children by losing many crucial employment rights, even when they were lucky enough to resume work with the same employer. Taking time off meant losing all previous seniority rights and the benefits that go with this — such as sickness benefit, pension rights, redundancy entitlements and so on. And the Employment Protection Act *has not fully remedied* this unfair situation. The Act only guarantees the employee the right to pick up from where she left off, maybe over 7 months previously, and does not place any obligation on the employer to count the time off as part of a continuous period of service when assessing pension rights and so on.

For all these reasons, negotiated maternity leave agreements that improve on the legal minima are a *must* for trade unionists. Here are some points to go for in negotiations —

- maternity leave available to part-timers
- a qualifying period shorter than 2 years
- a longer period of paid leave — some agreements give 18 weeks
- the 'right to return' to be extended up to, say one year.
- full continuity of employment in respect of pension rights and so on.
- leave without loss of pay to attend ante-natal clinics.
- provision for part-time work at full salary for a short period after return to work.
- paternity leave of say one week.

An important issue to watch in agreements is whether paid maternity leave is counted against sick pay. There is no reason why it should be. Pregnancy is not an illness!

Another point to consider for inclusion in an agreement is 'family responsibility' leave. Why should a man or woman having to take time off to look after a sick child be forced to subtract this from their own sick leave or holiday entitlement? In Poland, either parent can take time off on full pay to care for a sick child. In 1974 in Sweden a law was introduced giving either parent a right to up to ten days leave a year to look after a sick child. Why wait for the law in this country? This is a good area for negotiation.

So too is the area of extended leave for *fathers* to look after their children. We need to think in terms of 'child-rearing' leave for both sexes with right of return provisions.

Creche and nursery facilities

We have already seen that maternity leave can mean little in practice if a woman cannot find the nursery facilities that enable her to return to work. And in spite of the current concern with equality for women, the number of local authority day nurseries has actually *declined*. In 1946 there were 1,300 nurseries; in 1975 there were 453. Many unions have policies calling for the state to provide free care for all pre-school children whose mothers are working. But adequate state provision will clearly be a long-term objective. What can we do now?

This is what the NALGO Equal Rights Working Party has to say on this question —

'Coupled with improved maternity leave provisions the Working Party wants to see a comprehensive expansion of nurseries and childcare facilities. This should be provided as part of the state education service but clearly in the short term this is unlikely and efforts should therefore be concentrated on persuading employers to provide facilities'.

A TUC report on provisions for the Under Fives expressed a similar view.

What problems can you see with employer-provided creche facilities?
— company nurseries can keep women tied to their jobs and restrict their mobility and freedom of choice.

— company nurseries can depress wages; knowing a woman is tied to her job, employers can keep pay at a lower rate than that paid for comparable work elsewhere.

— employers may try to provide facilities on the cheap, against the interests of both the children and the nursery workers.

How valid do you think are these objections?

It could be argued that *all* good terms and conditions of employment 'tie' workers to their jobs, in that they would not do as well elsewhere. The union response here should be to make sure that all terms of conditions and employment are nearer to 'best practice'. Similarly it should be up to union negotiators to ensure that employers do *not* use nurseries to depress wages or to exploit nursery workers.

Most company nurseries that exist were set up solely at the initiative of management in order to attract and retain scarce female labour. And clearly if creches are totally in the hands of management there is the danger that some managers would use them for their interests alone. That is why it is important that the provision of creche facilities at work becomes a subject of *negotiation*. And there is evidence that this is beginning to happen. A questionnaire by the TUC Under Fives Working Party found that APEX has successfully negotiated the establishment of 6 workplace nurseries.

Where there is not sufficient demand in one work place to justify nursery facilities, then unions can explore the establishment of joint nurseries, catering for the employees of several work places in close proximity. Joint nurseries may also mean that a woman is less tied to one place of work.

Here are some of the steps involved in negotiating for a nursery:

● assessing demand within your workplace.

● contacting other workplaces that might be interested in joint nurseries.

● finding suitable premises within the workplace or in the neighbourhood. (Local authorities can often help here, and must be contacted to find out what sort of premises are needed to meet local authority requirements). One factor you will need to bear in mind is public transport facilities between workplaces, nursery premises and housing estates.

● doing costings for the nursery — an important element here will be staffing costs. Local authorities will tell you the approved ratios of staff to children and the local authority rates of pay for staff. (It is important that workplace nurseries are not run 'on the cheap', harming children and staff. If you are going to pay your staff adequate wages it is hard to run a nursery for less than £20 per child per week — at 1977 prices).

● your aim will be to get substantial employer subsidisation of this cost. If you do not think your employer would pay a full subsidy you could negotiate for an employer subsidy of two thirds of the cost per child. As well as day to day running costs there will also be initial start-up costs in terms of modifying buildings, buying equipment, and so on. If the employer will not agree to provide this money, grants or loans might be obtained from your local authority.

● deciding who runs the creche. If it is a negotiated facility, this should not be left to management. Representatives of unions and parents should be involved. The TUC and other unions such as the GMWU, have a policy that local authorities should be involved in the administration of work place creches, to alleviate management domination and ensure effective standards. So it is worth enquiring if your local authority would be interested in places on the management committee.

Does your union have a policy on nursery facilities? How would you argue to your workmates that nursery facilities should be taken up as a negotiating issue?

Improving the position of part-time women

The questionnaire at the beginning of the chapter asked about part-time women at your workplace. Too often these women get overlooked, but until there are adequate nursery facilities. many women who need to work will have no option but to work part-time. And indeed some women may prefer to work part-time to have more time with their children. The question is whether they should so often have to pay the price for this of losing out on employment rights and promotion, and being trapped in the bottom grade jobs.

These are the only kinds of jobs that employers usually consider 'suitable' for part-time work. Some employers may see the provision of special 'Mums' shifts that fit in with school hours as a way of keeping wages down. The NALGO working party found that 50% of all part-time members were in the bottom pay grade earning less than £1000, and 80% were in the bottom two grades. What can negotiators do about this?

● Ensure that all part-timers are union members and that their problems are treated as seriously as full-timers.

● Explore the possibility of adapting jobs which management normally regards as full-time jobs so that they can be shared by women on a part-time basis through 'job-sharing' or 'job pairing'.

● Explore the possibilities of flexitime which would enable women to work full-time and still fit in with family responsibilities.

Job-pairing
means that two women divide one full-time job with equal responsibility for the whole job. The job is covered full-time either by a morning/afternoon or 2½ days each split. In some cases jobs are divided on an alternate weeks basis (e.g. Barclays Bank). Pairing can carry over into domestic arrangements — whoever is off looks after the other children.

Job sharing
is also a system for dividing a full-time job but each woman is responsible for only half the work. This can work where responsibility for specific projects or clients can be arranged. The Civil Service has made quite extensive experiments in this area.

 Do you think job sharing, job pairing or flexi-time could be applied in your work place?

Do you think they would raise any problems for the unions?

Do you think job sharing and job pairing should be negotiated for men, so that they can spend more time with their children?

Training
The reason why most women are clustered at the bottom of the jobs ladder is that they lack the training to do more skilled jobs. The disturbing fact is that in spite of equality legislation, there are now *fewer* skilled women workers than there were in 1911!

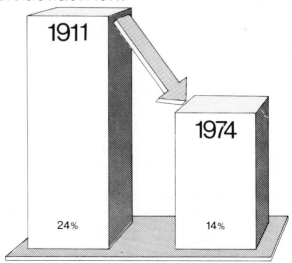

1911   1974

24%   14%

It is often said that our schools should do more to attack the attitudes that lie at the roots of this problem, but the attitude that women don't *need* training for a career still continues after school. For example a TUC report on 'The Roots of Inequality' discussed at the 1972 Womens Conference had this to say about day release provisions:

'The overall position is that 10.4 per cent of young women in employment receive day-release (compared with 39.7 per cent of young men) but if national and local government are excluded the proportion of young women falls to 8.9 per cent.'

What are the figures on day release for your firm?

Do you have an agreement with management on education and training, specifying the terms and conditions on which *all* workers have a right to day-release training?

The same picture emerges from apprenticeship figures. In 1973 7% of girls went into apprenticeships compared to 42% of boys; over three quarters of all apprenticeships for girls were in hairdressing.

Does your firm do apprentice training?

Have you ever thought of discussing with management how more women could be taken on as apprentices?

In 1976 the Engineering Industry Training Board decided to provide financial incentives to encourage employers to do just this. The plan, to train 100 girls in engineering over a two-year period, was estimated to cost £500,000. Employers are given a grant as an incentive to take on the girl apprentices in their second year for on-the-job training. In a report on training for women the Training Services Agency proposed providing incentives to selected employers for first year off-the-job training for a number of girl engineering technician trainees.

Could your firm fall within such a scheme?

Is there an ITB covering your occupation?

Has it made any recommendations for more effective training of women?

Training is an area where *positive discrimination* can play an important role. And here again the Sex Discrimination Act allows for single-sex training courses where the object is to train women to do jobs that have previously been 'mens jobs'. Training provisions of this kind could well become a topic for negotiations within a firm, leading to arguments that a specified quota of women be trained for 'mens jobs'.

Equal but different?
'But can women do men's jobs?' might be the response from management or fellow-trade unionists — 'they couldn't do the heavy work and anyway men and women are just better at different kinds of jobs.'

How would you answer these kinds of arguments?

Points to remember
● Women did all kinds of men's jobs in munition factories during the war.
● technological developments increasingly make the 'stength' argument

irrelevant. The fact that many jobs are still regarded today as 'men's jobs' may simply be a hang-over from the days when considerable strength was needed to do particular jobs by hand — jobs which nowadays are done by machines.

● research has shown that different abilities between men and women in terms of say manual dexterity or mathematical tasks are in fact very slight. Could many of these differences even today be explained by differences of training and education — such as boys getting mechanical toys while girls are encouraged to do needlework or knitting?

Protective laws

You often hear the argument that if women want to do men's work they must take the good with the bad. They must be prepared to do shift work, night work and high levels of overtime. This would mean abolishing the 'protective laws' laid down in various Factories Acts which at present shield women from such kinds of work except where special exemptions are granted.

These protective laws can at present be a reason for women being ousted from skilled jobs, if management wants these jobs performed on a 24 hour basis.

Some people argue that these laws should be repealed if we are to have full equality (employers have argued strongly for their repeal). Others argue that the responsibilities of parenthood and dometic work are *not* yet shared equally. The main burden still falls on women. If they are under more pressure to work anti-social hours, many of them will suffer and so will their children. And of course the other argument is that the protective laws should be *extended* to apply to men — if these working conditions are bad for women, then they are bad for men too. Equality should never be achieved at the expense of one group *losing* rights.

 What is your view on this question?

Using an equal opportunity clause

An essential starting point for fighting sex discrimination in your workplace is to have an equal opportunities clause in your agreement. This is the model clause recommended by the TUC:

'The parties to this agreement are committed to the development of positive policies to promote equal opportunity in employment regardless of worker's sex, marital status, creed, colour, race or ethnic origins. This principle will apply in respect of all conditions of work including pay, hours of work, holiday entitlement, overtime and shiftwork, work allocation, guaranteed earnings, sick pay, pensions, recruitment, training, promotion and redundancy. The management undertake to draw opportunities for training and promotion to the attention of all eligible employees, and to inform all employees of this Agreement on equal opportunity.

The parties agree that they will review from time to time, through their joint machinery, the operation of this equal opportunity policy.

If any employee considers that he or she is suffering from unequal treatment on the grounds of sex, marital status, creed, colour, race or ethnic origins he or she may make a complaint which will be dealt with through the agreed procedure for dealing with grievances'.

If you really make use of such a clause, it will be a much more effective protection against discrimination than recourse to the law. To make such a clause work, you will need to scrutinise fully *all* existing agreements, especially those covering pensions, sick pay, fringe benefits, redundancy procedures. Do these discriminate in any way against women? It is important here to recognise *indirect* as well as *direct* discrimination. For example, even if an agreement does not say 'these fringe benefits are not available to women' but says rather 'these fringe benefits are available to workers only in grades 1 and 2', then this can *still be discriminatory* against women if all or most women are in grades 3 and 4. The Sex Discrimination Act outlaws both kinds of discrimination. But indirect discrimination is always harder to spot than direct discrimination.

The *regular monitoring of progress* will also need to be a key part of the operation of such a clause. To do this you will need a regular supply of information from management on recruitment, promotion, training and wage rates broken down by sex. In areas where women still seem to lag behind it will be important to discuss with management measures for overcoming this — perhaps by negotiating fixed 'quotas' of women for recruitment training and promotion, where this would be practicable.

The GMWU adds the following note to the TUC equal opportunities clause in their guide to Negotiators:

'Negotiators are advised to ensure that the operation of the equality clause does not allow the protective legislation provisions to be contravened and provisions to this effect should be included in the collective agreements concerned'.

Action check list

● Discuss with women members whether your branch or workplace meetings be held at more convenient times.

● Consider whether you need to negotiate for the right to hold workplace meetings during working hours, with pay.

● Start a discussion in your branch about providing creche facilities at branch meetings.

● Consider whether it would be useful to set up a special sub-committee in your branch or at your workplace to do research and propaganda on women's rights and organisation in the area.

● Consider a union recruiting campaign among part-time workers.

● Consider whether resolutions to your branch on the following issues could help the interests of your women members:

1 asking that your NEC set up a special working party to do research into the position of women members within the union and at work.

2 asking that your union provides creche facilities at its next delegate conference.

3 asking that your union reserves a number of seats on its executive specially for women.

4 asking that your union set up a national committee against discrimination.

● If such a committee exists in your union, find out what it is doing, and who the representative on it is from your branch, district or division.

● Find out what training opportunities are open to your union's women members in practice.

● Discuss negotiating an equal opportunity clause in your agreement.

● As well as such a clause, should you get management to agree to supply regular information broken down by sex on wage rates, occupations, recruitment, training and any other questions relevant to fighting sex discrimination in your firm?

● Discuss with your fellow shop stewards the need to negotiate a maternity leave agreement.

● Discuss with your fellow shop stewards whether there is a need for negotiating nursery facilities at your workplace.

● Would flexi-time, or job sharing help part time women and also men who might want to spend more time with their families?

● Could training and day release opportunities for women be improved through negotiations?

● Could you arrange a showing of the TU Studies films: 'Equal Pay' and 'Sisters and Brothers' as a stimulus to discussion of issues like these at your union branch? (To obtain them, see pp 182-3).

Further Reading
General
'Equal Pay' chapter in Trade Union Studies Book 1 (see pp 183).
'Organising Women Workers' Judith Hunt, WEA Studies for Trade Unionists Vol 1, No. 3.
'Women and Work: Manpower papers Nos. 9-12 HMSO
'Training Opportunities for Women' Training Services Agency, HMSO 1975.

Union Surveys and Policy Guides
NALGO 'Equal Rights Working Party' 1975.
ACTT 'Patterns of Discrimination Against Women in the Film and Television Industries' 1975
GMWU 'Equality at Work — the Way Forward: A Guide for Negotiators' 1976
TASS 'Womens Rights and What we Are Doing to Get Them' 1975

Maternity leave and nurseries
'Maternity Rights for Working Women' Jean Coussins NCCL 1976.
'Maternity Leave' Incomes Data Services Study No. 100 June 1975.
Labour Research, April 1976, April 1977.
'Child Care at Work' Incomes Data Services Study No. 129 Sept. 1976.

Chapter 5   Company Pensions — Who Cares?

Why are we including a chapter on Pensions in a book on Industrial Democracy? In Chapter One we saw that one of the aims of the unions is to extend collective bargaining on conditions of employment to include occupational pension schemes. In the past a service pension has sometimes been seen as a sort of gift from the employer as a 'reward for good service'. Often a pension with the job was associated with 'staff' conditions for a 'privileged' group of workers — frequently not in unions. But to the employer who is making pension contributions, these become something that can be seen as part of the overall wage bill — and, of course, no one would claim that wages were simply a gift.

This chapter is not designed to give guidelines to negotiating a 'good' occupational pension scheme. (Some helpful notes on this can be found in the TUC book 'Occupational Pension Schemes — a TUC Guide'; you should also ask about courses run by the TUC or your own union for pension negotiators or pension trustees.) Rather, this chapter looks at pensions chiefly from the point of view of industrial democracy — that is to say the application of collective bargaining in the setting up of a scheme, and member participation in running a scheme.

For workers who are already, or about to be, members of occupational pension schemes there are some very important issues for democracy at work. These include:

1 who decides on the rules of the pension scheme

2 who controls and manages the scheme

3 how are changes in contributions and benefits decided

Trade unionists should also include another item in discussion about company pensions — their relationship to the state scheme.

One of the general objectives that unions have is to ensure a decent level of income in retirement for *all* workers — and that means examining the relationship between the State scheme and occupational schemes. Some trade unionists may even decide that the insecurity and problems attached to occupational schemes should lead them to reject them altogether. Others will conclude that the best solution is to run an occupational scheme in harness with the new state scheme.

At the present time (1977) there are a large number of negotiations taking place about pension schemes. This is because when the new earnings-related state scheme comes into operation in April 1978, each individual employer with an occupational scheme will have to have made the decision on whether its members should be 'contracted-out' or whether they should pay the additional National Insurance payments that would entitle them to an earnings-related state pension. The legislation which introduced the new state earnings-related pension scheme also required the employer running a private occupational pension scheme to consult with the recognised unions about the contracting out decision and then to inform all employees. Trade unionists will, naturally, want to see that this means proper negotiations on the pension issue. The basic features of the contracting-out decision are explained further in the TUC booklet, 'Trade Unions and Contracting Out'.

79

Questions

Note down your answers to these questions before watching the television programme or working through the chapter.

1 Does your employer have —

☐ no pension scheme at all
☐ a pension scheme that covers certain employees
☐ a pension scheme that covers all employees.

2 If your employer runs a pension scheme, is it —

☐ contracted out of the earnings-related part of the new State scheme
☐ not contracted out
☐ no decision has been finalised on contracting out.

3 Are negotiations currently taking place between your union and your employer on —

☐ the rules of your pension scheme
☐ contributions to the scheme
☐ benefits under the scheme.

4 Do you have a copy of — or ready access to —

☐ a members booklet explaining the scheme
☐ the scheme rules
☐ the latest annual accounts of the scheme
☐ the latest valuation report on the scheme.

5 Are the trustees of your pension scheme —

☐ all appointed by management
☐ all elected by the membership
☐ half appointed by your employer and half by the membership
☐ appointed by some other method.

6 If you have a pension scheme does it cover —

☐ just the plant/site/office you work in
☐ all plants owned by your employer
☐ several employers in the industry you work in.

7 Does your union negotiate about pensions —

☐ through the usual bargaining arrangements
☐ through special bargaining arrangements.

These questions raise the basic issues about the trade union approach to pension schemes, and their implications for industrial democracy.

Why have occupational pension schemes?

We do not necessarily assume in this chapter that an OPS is the best way of providing income in retirement. We need to get several points clear right from the outset:

● It is a key trade union objective that there should be an adequate State pension as part of comprehensive social security provision. If large numbers of employers indicate that they will contract out of the new State earnings-related pension arrangements due to start in 1978, then this could seriously affect the adequacy of State pensions during the first years of the new scheme's life.

● To the individual member of a pension scheme, contributions are just a form of saving for retirement. The advantages of using an employment-based pension scheme in preference to other methods of saving have to be set against the disadvantages.

● Too often an occupational scheme is seen as an *alternative* to the earnings-related part of the new State scheme. Because of the question marks that hang over the value of benefits under occupational schemes, however, many trade unionists would prefer to see them used to 'top up' the State scheme. This would allow the occupational scheme to provide some of the additional benefits not available under the State scheme at present — such as lump sum payments at retirement age. Under this sort of arrangement a retiring worker would have three sources of pension benefit —

Occupational pension

State earnings-related pension

Basic State pension

● In the TUC guide to trade unions on making the contracting out decision the TUC stress the need to take a long term view. Arrangements that may seem perfectly adequate at one point in time can be completely wrecked by inflation and fundamental economic and industrial changes. A pension scheme member just commencing in a scheme this year could well be receiving pension payments well into the middle of the 21st century. The TUC guide makes these comments about this situation:

'It would be foolhardy to expect the new State scheme to remain unchanged for all of that period and the changes made can be of advantage either to those who contracted out or to those who did not contract out'.

The TUC guide then goes on to give an example from recent pensions history which illustrates clearly how political and economic changes can radically affect the wisdom of decisions about pensions. The example is the now defunct Graduated Pension Scheme, first set up in 1965:

'This was wound up in April 1975, but graduated pensions already earned in that scheme will in future be protected against inflation. This protection is not to be given to the equivalent pension benefits due to those members of private occupational pension schemes that were contracted out of part of the State graduated scheme. If those who decided to contract out had known that there would be such an important change, very much to the advantage of those who did not contract out, their decision, probably, would have been very different.'

The TUC goes on —

'Equally with the new scheme, if it is thought that future changes will favour those who do not contract out, this is a powerful argument in favour of participating fully in the state scheme'.

The TUC's view, then, is broadly in favour of contracting in. However, some individual unions, such as ASTMS, have considered the matter through their own research offices and are advising their members to contract out. This could be simply because they believe that, as things stand at the moment, an occupational pension scheme offers better benefits than the state scheme; they may, especially in the case of white-collar unions, have a large number of members in occupational pension schemes which have already been the subject of collective bargaining in setting up the scheme, and they may feel that the existence of a properly negotiated scheme with member participation in *running* the scheme is an important way of extending industrial democracy.

Collective Bargaining and pensions

In the rest of this chapter we make the assumption that we are talking about private occupational schemes. There is a basic difference between the State scheme and some public service schemes, which operate on what is known as a 'pay-as-you-go system', and virtually all private sector schemes, which are 'funded'. The diagrams opposite will help you to see the difference.

In a pay-as-you-go scheme there is no accumulated pension fund: the pension contributions of today's wage earners and employers pay for today's pensioners. Under this system contributions go up automatically as earnings increase, and so an inflation adjustment is built into the system. A fund can be dispensed with because of the security of State backing.

In a funded scheme, contributions go into an investment fund which will include shares and interest-bearing loans. Pensions will be paid in due course from those contributions plus the income received through dividends paid on the shares and interest on the loans. Every so often the value of the fund will be reassessed to take account of changes in share values. The total value of the fund might go up or down, depending on the state of the stock market and the general economic climate.

**Pay as you
go scheme**

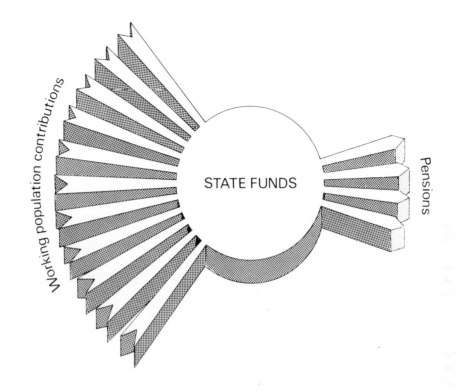

Working population contributions

STATE FUNDS

Pensions

Funded scheme

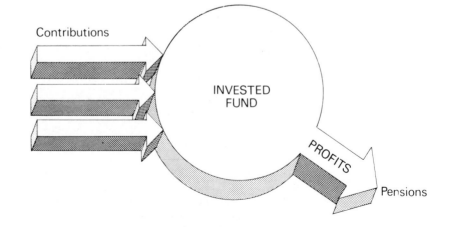

Contributions

INVESTED
FUND

PROFITS

Pensions

Inevitably there will be more negotiating issues for unions dealing with private funded schemes because of the need for union safeguards over the adequacy of the fund, the contributions to it and the benefits from it, and the powers of the trustees associated with it.

But the important thing is to establish firmly that pensions is a negotiating issue, just like any other.

Active trade unionists will be familiar with a distinction made between two types of agreements negotiated between unions and employers —

procedure agreements
and
substantive agreements

The first type is about union recognition and facilities, and procedures for dealing with issues such as disputes and grievances, health and safety questions, job security, disclosure of information, etc. The second type, substantive agreements, deals with the actual terms and conditions of employment — wages, hours, holidays, sick pay, maternity leave etc. We can use this idea of two types of negotiations when thinking about pensions —

Procedural negotiations about the way the scheme is set up, how contributions and benefits are decided, how the scheme's trustees are appointed, how the scheme is managed.

Substantive negotiations about the level of contributions by employees and employer, the scheme's benefits, and the scheme rules.

All of these items are negotiable. The key issue for unions is whether these issues at the moment *are* negotiated, or whether on the other hand they are left in the hands of management or 'experts' from the pensions industry.

In this chapter it will be impossible to go into any detail about pension scheme contributions and benefits, but some basic principles need to be discussed.

Contributions and Benefits

We mentioned in the Introduction to this chapter the problem of pensions being seen as a 'gift' from the employer, rather than a genuine bargaining issue. You may have heard people say that pensions are different because both sides — employers and employees — make contributions to the pension fund; so pensions are really a mutual arrangement rather than a bargaining issue. But we can look at the issue of pension contributions in another way. To an employer, once he has decided to introduce a scheme, pension contributions become another cost to add to other labour costs. The diagram (opposite) makes this clear.

By viewing it this way both employer and employee contributions to the pension fund come ultimately from the same source — the employer's total labour costs.

Now, this analysis raises two important points for trade unionists:

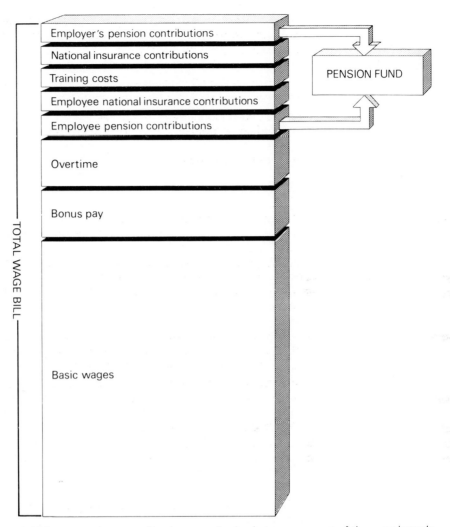

Employer's pension contributions

National insurance contributions

Training costs

Employee national insurance contributions

Employee pension contributions

PENSION FUND

Overtime

Bonus pay

Basic wages

TOTAL WAGE BILL

1 When pension contributions are looked at as one part of the employer's total labour costs, then it can be argued that negotiations on pensions should be treated with the same importance as other labour cost items — such as basic wage rates, overtime and shift rates, sick pay, maternity pay, etc.

2 Pensions should be seen as part of the total package of benefits that unions negotiate about; in other words unions might decide to go for a bigger increase in pensions and give less emphasis to some other benefit — or vice-versa.

This last idea has led some trade unionists to put forward a different view about pensions. Occupational pensions, they would say, should really be seen as a decision by workers to set aside some of the present wage bill to put into a fund for the future. In other words, the union negotiators would decide that some of the employer's labour costs should be paid into a pension fund. If there was no pension fund, so the argument goes, then this money might be available to improve other wages or conditions of employment. You will sometimes hear this argument referred to in the

PENSION

phrase 'Pensions are really deferred wages' (ie wages that workers have decided to accept in the form of pension contributions).

The TUC put it this way in their guide to negotiations on pension schemes:

'The importance of trade union negotiation on the terms of an occupational pension scheme cannot be overemphasised. The money paid into a pension scheme is part of the earnings of the members of the scheme which they have chosen to put aside for their future use'.

The TUC went on—

'This concept of occupational pension schemes has two important implications. First, that consideration of negotiations on the pension scheme cannot be divorced from that on negotiations on other earnings.' We have already looked at this point when we talked about the need for unions to take a 'total package' approach to wages and conditions.

The second important implication described by the TUC is —

'that the money that is actually to be paid into the pension scheme is the basic variable in the negotiations.'

This point seems fairly obvious, and yet it carries major implications for pension negotiations. The reason is that it is customary for unions not to concentrate on how much the employer pays into the scheme, but instead to negotiate about the benefits that members of the scheme can expect. This position — in which the union negotiates the benefits to be made available under the scheme but not the contributions to be paid by the employer — seems to carry the immediate advantages that the members of the scheme can be reasonably certain of the benefits they will get at retirement, and that any shortfalls in the fund would have to be made up by the employer. The TUC, however, identified some serious drawbacks to this approach. They were —

● bargaining on the details of a pension scheme can be a long-drawn out affair; and pensions experts often have a great deal of say. On the other hand, negotiating over the total contribution to the fund is straightforward: it simply requires a compromise agreement somewhere between what the union wants and what the employer claims he can afford

● if only the benefits are negotiated, then this strengthens the employer's argument that what he puts into the scheme and how it is invested is no concern of the members. From the Industrial Democracy standpoint, this would of course be very unsatisfactory.

● employers will throughout the life of the scheme object to improvements on the ground that they would cost him too much. Union negotiators will therefore be put under great pressure by employers to accept poorly funded schemes

● any surplus that arises when the fund is revalued would lead to the employer reducing his contributions, whereas the employee contributions would remain the same.

The alternative to just negotiating about benefits is put forward in the TUC Guide's chapter on Pension Negotiations — 'An alternative approach is to negotiate basically on the current rate of total joint contribution to the scheme.' Under this approach the agreement might specify that total contributions would be 15% of earnings, for example.

The TUC goes on —

'In the actual negotiations a fixed contribution approach simplifies the collective bargaining tremendously, all that is negotiated is what the employer can pay. Clearly it is necessary to have an indication of the cost of the various benefits, so that the general shape of the scheme can be determined in relation to a particular rate of contribution. Once that rate is determined, discussion can move on to the details, but, since these will affect the cost to the employer, he will have less reason to interfere. Further, any surplus money that arises will not flow back to the employer.'

Clearly under this approach unions would have to take more responsibility for the rate of contributions, and the pension fund itself rather than the employer would have to bear the effect of any deficits that appeared through revaluation. But two other points need to be made about this contribution approach suggested by the TUC —

● Negotiations on this approach would be about cash the employer has, and not about future promises he might fulfill. This would strengthen the union's attempts to make pensions a genuine collective bargaining issue.

● If you review carefully the points made above about these two approaches, it seems clear that negotiating about *contributions* to the scheme, rather than detailed scheme *benefits* in the initial stages, would mean that subsequently the union would have more say in decisions about benefit details. The union would also be able to have much more say in the running of the scheme, and the employer would not be able to reduce his contributions if surpluses occurred; instead these could be used for the benefit of the members.

Do your pension scheme rules fix the amount of contribution to be paid by the employer — or only the amount to be paid by the scheme members?

Which approach does your union favour for pension negotiations?

Benefit details

It is impossible in this chapter for us to describe detailed objectives for unions when looking at pension scheme details. If you are concerned about this you should get a copy of the TUC guide to Occupational Pension Schemes, which contains a 'model scheme' you will find very helpful.

One general point needs to be made, however. You will sometimes hear it said that pension schemes have to vary in the benefits they can offer because of the particular circumstances of an industry or company. While this will be true in particular cases, you need to bear in mind the general point that the *maximum benefits* a scheme may provide are governed by a set of rules drawn up by the Inland Revenue for tax relief purposes; pension schemes may not exceed the benefits under these rules, otherwise tax relief will be lost on members' contributions and dividends and interest paid into the pension scheme fund. These maximum benefits are described in the TUC guide. So the *actual benefits* that a scheme can provide will be determined by the funding of the scheme — in other words pension benefits should be decided by the union-employer negotiations on how much the employer is to pay into the fund.

We will now move on to look at the *procedural* side of pension negotiations.

Who controls the pension scheme?

This is the basic question for unions when looking at the industrial democracy aspect of pensions. So far we have been looking at some of the issues involved in making pensions a live collective bargaining issue. We now need to look briefly at some of the implications for union-management procedures, and trade union organisation.
The first issue we look at is information.

Pension scheme information

A recurrent theme in this book is the need for unions to have adequate information to lay a sound basis for collective bargaining. The TUC's guide suggests a list of relevant information for unions negotiating on pensions. You might like to check the information currently available to you against that list.

Controlling the scheme

Pension schemes normally have a board of trustees. Their functions include supervising the investment policy, deciding to pay or not to pay certain benefits in the scheme which are discretionary (eg dependants' benefits), arranging for valuations of the scheme, and giving advice to members (such as, what to do with a lump sum paid at retirement, for example). Trustees functions are limited by law — in particular they are obliged to administer the fund in the best interests of the members. This may need to be balanced against any personal scruples they may have about certain types of investment.
The terms of the Trust Deed governing the scheme should be a subject of collective bargaining.
Clearly the functions of pensions trustees are crucial for the control of the scheme, and the union objective has been put forward in the TUC guide:

'The scheme should be run jointly by the employers and the employees through their trade unions, and, in particular, the membership of boards of trustees or management should be split, *with the employers having at the most 50 per cent representation*.'

The TUC goes on —

'If a situation arises which cannot be resolved within the scheme it will be necessary to use normal collective bargaining'.

This relationship between normal collective bargaining procedures and the role of union appointed pension trustees is crucial. It is a central objective of unions to make sure that they have at least a 50/50 say — if not majority control — in the management of the scheme through the trustees.
Control of the scheme through the composition of the trustees board is itself a matter to be negotiated between unions and the employer.

Bargaining procedures and union organisation

Why have pension negotiations been such a problem for many unions? It is clearly the case that effective union control over pension schemes is lacking in a great many cases.

One of the important factors behind this is the fact that in most cases pension negotiations will need to be conducted at the level of the company as a unit. Often collective bargaining machinery and union organisation at this level is very weak. This diagram helps to make the point:

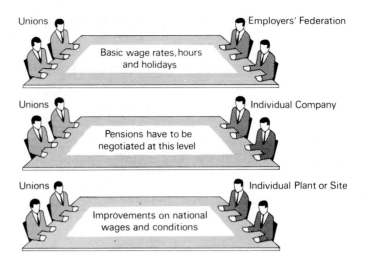

Unions — Employers' Federation
Basic wage rates, hours and holidays

Unions — Individual Company
Pensions have to be negotiated at this level

Unions — Individual Plant or Site
Improvements on national wages and conditions

You can see that it may be the case that pension negotiations are cut off from other bread-and-butter negotiating issues because they take place at company level and not at the level of the whole industry or the individual plant. If your union is accustomed to negotiating at these levels, it may be that union organisation between different plants in the company is relatively weak.

This issue is so important that we take the whole of the next chapter to discuss it. Once again, we must stress the point that without effective union organisation a real increase in industrial democracy is virtually meaningless.

Action checklist
● Make sure you have a complete set of the information you need about your pension scheme, as set out on page 80.

● Discuss the current state of play on pension negotiations with your union colleagues, using the materials in this chapter. One way of raising interest and stimulating discussion would be to obtain the TU Studies film 'Company Pensions — who Cares?' to show to your committee or branch (to obtain it, see pp 183).

● Investigate what courses are run by your union and the TUC for pension trustees and negotiators.

Further references
The basic sources of reference we have quoted from in this chapter have been the TUC booklets 'Occupational Pension Schemes' and 'Trade Unions and Contracting Out', available from the TUC bookshop.

Other publications you should collect are the free Department of Health and Social Security leaflets, the most important of which is 'Family Benefits and Pensions'.

A detailed guide to maximum tax allowable pension benefits is 'Occupational Pension Scheme, Notes on approval under the Finance Act 1970'. This is available from the joint office of the Superannuation Funds Office of the Inland Revenue, and the Occupational Pensions Board:

Apex Tower, High Street, New Malden, Surrey, KT3 4DN.

Chapter 6   Too Big To Bargain With?

As we saw earlier, extending collective bargaining doesn't just mean bringing new issues into existing bargaining machinery. In order to deal properly with some new issues there may be a need for new bargaining machinery at higher levels of large organisations. Previous chapters have given us examples of a number of issues that can't be tackled properly just at work place level if your work place is also part of a large organisation. Effective policies on health and safety and job design mean that workers need to influence their employer's policies on investment and product development; union policies on issues like pensions and equal opportunities will often be most effective if co-ordinated and standardised over an organisation as a whole.

In this chapter we are looking at large employers generally, whether they are giant private companies, nationalised industries or public services, and we refer to all these 'Giants' as 'organisations'. Because of the sheer size of all these organisations, workers will face very similar problems in terms of coping with complex management decision-making structures.

As organisations get larger, decision making becomes increasingly centralised — major decisions on future plans that affect your work place are taken further and further away from the work place. The key question is therefore, how do trade unionists need to organise in order to influence these issues, without themselves becoming too centralised and less democratic? This is what this chapter seeks to explore by looking at the structure of large organisations, where different kinds of decisions are taken, and the implications of this for trade union organisation.

Questions

Note down your answers to these questions before watching the television programme or working through the chapter.

1 Does your organisation as a whole employ

less than 5,000 ☐   more than 5,000 ☐   more than 10,000 ☐

Yes No

☐ ☐ **2** Have management at your work place ever said to you that they lack authority to deal with a particular issue, because the decision is taken at a higher level of the organisation?

☐ ☐ **3** Do you exchange information with shop stewards at other work places that are part of your organisation?

☐ ☐ **5** Do you have regular meetings with shop stewards from other work places in your organisation?

☐ ☐ **5** Are these meetings given official recognition or support by your union?

6 Do you have meetings with levels of management outside your particular work place?

☐ Never

☐ When there is a crisis

☐ Regularly

7 Do you know if your full time officials have regular meetings with management at higher levels of the organisation?

☐ ☐

8 Does your union have a policy on joint shop steward or combine committees?

☐ ☐

Issues for the chapter

After working through the chapter you should have a clearer idea of:

1 How large organisations make decisions.

2 How unions can organise to be more effective in challenging top management decisions.

The Private Sector
The emergence of the giants

There is a trend for fewer and fewer companies to account for a larger and larger proportion of Britain's total production. At present the top 100 firms account for about 50% of total manufacturing output. The Bullock Report has this to say about a survey of the top 1,000 enterprises:

'Only 1 in 5 of them employs under 1,000 people; nearly two thirds of them employ 2,000 or more people; and there are 155 enterprises with 10,000 or more UK employees.'
Report of the Bullock Committee of Inquiry on Industrial Democracy, HMSO January 1977

And of course many of these organisations are multinational in their operations, with employees overseas as well.

The Bullock report estimated that over 7 million people out of a total of 18 million people in the private sector are employed by large enterprises. Particularly important is the fact that virtually all these large enterprises are in fact *groups* of companies, organised in pyramids of holding and subsidiary companies.

What this means is that although the plant where you work may itself be fairly small, it might well be part of a bigger company, which in turn may itself be a subsidiary of an overall holding company. Companies at each level of the pyramid might well operate under quite different names, so the links are not always immediately obvious.

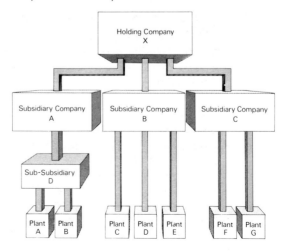

Assuming that you were employed in plant A, this means that important decisions affecting your work place would be taken at least three higher levels in the pyramid.

If you are not sure who owns your company you can find out by going to the reference section of your local library and looking at 'Who owns whom'. Library assistants will help you. Later in the chapter we return to the question of how you can find out such information.

The internal organisation of many large companies is based on product groups or divisions. For example Cadbury Schweppes, which employs 28,369 employees in the U.K. has five groups beneath the main board: overseas group, confectionery group, drinks group, tea and foods group, and health and chemical products group. Within each of these product groups there are a large number of separate plants in different parts of the country.

Some companies may have a mixed structure of product divisions and subsidiaries with divisions closely controlled by the central board and subsidiaries having somewhat more autonomy. One example of this is ICI.

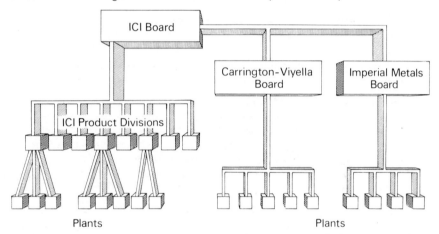

Plants   Plants

It will be important for workers in a subsidiary company of a large enterprise to know just how much freedom their subsidiary is allowed to determine its own plans, and how much decision making is centralised.

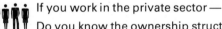 If you work in the private sector —
Do you know the ownership structure of your firm?

Do you have access to a diagram of your company showing how your plant relates to the top holding company through a structure of divisions or subsidiaries?

Public Sector

Nationalised Industries

The growth of large organisations has of course not been confined to the private sector. For example, the taking of industries into public ownership means the amalgamation of a number of separate firms into one large public corporation. The Iron and Steel Act of 1967 took into public ownership the assets and activities of fourteen companies, to form a new corporation employing over a quarter of a million people with plants located in all parts of the U.K. The new corporation had to develop a new management structure to ensure the necessary degree of centralised control and the structure that emerged was based on 6 product divisions, very much like some of the private industry structures we looked at earlier. There are nearly two million workers employed by large public corporations.

Public services

Within the public services too there have been similar developments in size and centralisation of power. Particularly important here was the re-organisation of Local Government and the Health Service in 1974. The idea was to create larger organisational units in order to boost efficiency and allow more effective centralised control over the planning of services and the allocation of resources within regions.

Within local government strategic planning is now carried out by the new and much larger county authorities with the district authorities responsible for implementing these plans and dealing with more local issues.
In the health service too we can find the same kind of decision making pyramid, with the ultimate power lying with the Government and underneath a structure of regional health authorities, area health authorities, district health authorities. Vital decisions affecting employees, say in a hospital, might be taken at all of these levels.

These changes in the organisation of public services affect a large number of trade unionists. There are nearly 3 million people employed by local authorities (including education); and nearly 2 million employed in central government (including the National Health Service and the Post Office). Chapter 8 deals in more detail with the problems facing trade unionists in the public sector seeking to influence forward planning and policy formation.

Coping with a large organisation (1)

Implications for union organisation

'Old tactics and old methods of organisation have to be overhauled and brought up to date to enable us to meet and overcome the latest developments of organisation from the employers side'.

This was written by two shop stewards over 50 years ago, but the essential trade union principle of constantly reviewing methods of organisation remains just as valid, if not more so, today.

The structures of most trade unions evolved in response to a very different industrial situation. Most unions for example have a strong district structure which links with the National Executive and this was adequate when industry was all locally based, but an important question to ask now is how far this situation has changed and whether trade unions need to modify their structures in order to cope more effectively with the growth of large-scale organisations.
The experience of the public employees' union NUPE is interesting here to give some idea of the issues involved and what can be achieved.

Following a debate on union re-organisation at NUPE's 1973 National Conference a research project was commissioned to look at —

'Possible changes in the structure of the Union which would take into account, not only the re-organisation of the Local Government, Health and

Water Services in April 1974, but also the continued growth and expansion of the Union and the need to maintain democracy and efficiency.'

One of the objectives of the re-organisation of NUPE was to provide a better system of organisation and policy-making to meet the new structure of management decision making in local government and the health service.

What the research report recommended was the establishment of Local Government and Health Service Districts within the union which would correspond to the relevant management and administrative authorities. Local Government Districts would be based upon the boundaries of Metropolitan Districts and County Districts. Health Service Districts would be based on the boundaries of District Health Authorities. Each of these districts would have a district committee of all the shop stewards and branch officials in the district. Committees would monitor local negotiations, liaise with full-time officials and send resolutions and delegates to committees at regional level. In this way the re-organisation would strengthen the links between work place activity and the union's decision making at higher levels.

The District Committee would be linked through the areas to National Committees which would have the job of monitoring national negotiations for each service and considering resolutions on negotiating policy. The new union organisation would therefore provide very concrete support for the extension of collective bargaining to higher levels of large organisations and enable hitherto fragmented shop stewards to match the increasing co-ordination of management organisation.

The proposals were adopted by the union with only minor amendments at a special conference in 1975.

Do you think that this kind of re-organisation of union structure to match management structure is only possible when a union deals with only a small number of very large employers?

Can you think of a situation outside the public service where such re-organisation might be possible?

Does the NUPE experience suggest to you any ideas that might be relevant to your union?

In some areas NUPE found that it was very difficult to organise properly because of the size of the area covered by management e.g. County Councils and Regional Water Authorities.

Would this be a problem for your union and the type of management structures it has to deal with?

The NUPE re-organisation was essentially an exercise in national level union re-structuring. But at the level of individual companies and organisations there is the question of how trade union representatives might need to adapt their own internal organisation to match more effectively the management decision making structure that they are trying to influence. Before trade unionists can decide what kind of organisation they need they will need to know at what level in the organisation various kinds of decisions are taken.

Coping with a large organisation (2)

Knowing where decisions are taken

Unions need to know where various decisions are taken so that they can be sure that when they meet management they are talking with the right people — with the people who have the authority and power to take action on the issue in question.

This is especially true where unions at present negotiate with personnel officers or industrial relations specialists, who have no authority over finance or production decisions and can only act as a 'go-between' to the members of management with the real decision making powers.

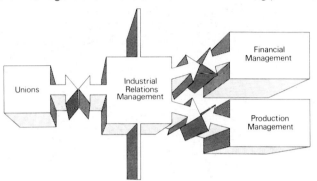

The TUC stressed this point in their 1975 Economic Review when discussing the extension of collective bargaining:

'Unions at present tend to deal with industrial relations specialists on the management side who do not have the responsibility for determining issues unions will want to bring within the scope of joint regulation'.

Precisely what decisions are taken at what levels will vary from organisation to organisation — there is no simple answer. But most large organisations in co-ordinating their operations follow some general management principles. The diagram below sets out how a fairly standard system of management planning and control would operate within the type of multi-plant company structures we looked at earlier.

The *corporate plan* establishes the company's overall objectives, answering essentially the following kinds of questions:

● what kind of business should the company be in?
● what kinds of products should it make?
● what kinds of markets are desired?
● what rate of growth is required?
● what are the profit targets?

The *financial plan* translates these overall objectives into financial terms. Detailed plans for each product division within the company will be produced, examining markets, product development, production facilities, personnel, materials, technical improvements, working capital. Detailed financial forecasts on costs, profits and capital expenditure will be made for each product division.

The setting of targets for each level of the organisation is sometimes referred to as *budgetary control system*. The targets set out in financial terms the responsibilities of managers at various levels in relation to overall company policy. Budgetary control operates by the continuous comparison of actual with target or budgeted results, so that if for example actual labour costs exceed budgeted costs, or actual production falls below budgeted targets, steps can be taken at the necessary level to correct these 'deviations'.

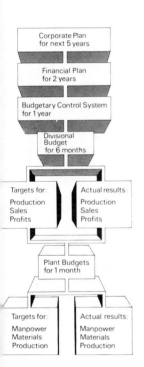

You can see from the diagrams that the targets for each level of the organisation are set *by the level of management above.* The system works by higher management checking to see whether lower levels of management have fulfilled company objectives.

Managers do of course have some autonomy to decide how to meet their targets. For example, a plant manager may have set figures for labour costs and output, but he will have the authority to decide how many workers in what categories of skill he employs for how many hours to meet these targets. It is important for you to find out exactly what freedom the managers you most come into contact with have to make decisions.

Implications for unions

1 Long term objectives on investment, product development and so on that will have effects on the job security, working environment and living standards of employees are established as part of the corporate plan, probably a number of years before the effects of these policies are experienced on the shop floor. Unless unions can influence the *early planning stages*, any subsequent influence they have can only be a question of minor adjustments to pre-set plans.

2 Division or product group level is an important level for trade union influence because it is here that overall financial objectives will begin to be translated into *actual* requirements of skills, machinery and so on. Effective union policies on recruitment, training, measures to avoid redundancies, retraining, or the job design and health and safety implications of new machinery, will require influence at this level.

3 Decisions taken by managers at each level are to a large extent pre-determined by targets set at a higher level. This means that a large number of problems *can't be solved at the level at which they arise* in large organisations. Unions need a procedure that gives them access to higher levels, and in a multi-plant company this means a procedure that goes beyond individual plants.

 Do you ever discuss the relation of actual performance to targets with your plant or workshop management?

Is there a corporate planning department in your organisation?

Do you have access to any information on the forward plans of your company?

—through written documents?

—through talks from senior management?

Corporate planning in the public service

In local government there has been a trend towards a similar corporate planning approach. The Bains report which examined management and structure in the new local authorities took the view that there was too much departmental fragmentation and that authorities should 'adopt a corporate approach to their affairs in order to ensure their resources are most effectively employed' (The New Local Authorities: Management and Structure, HMSO 1972). The Bains report advocated that there should be a policy and resouces committee in each authority which 'would aid the authority in setting objectives and priorities, and co-ordinating and controlling the implementation of those objectives and monitoring and reviewing performance.'

In other words it might be said that this committee would be involved in drawing up corporate and financial plans and a budgetary control system for the authority. This is a good illustration of the point that while the details of decision making and control structures in large organisations will vary enormously, there are a number of broad principles that apply more generally.

Coping with large organisations (3)

Strengthening Joint Union organisation

Most trade unionists recognise the importance of inter-union co-operation at the level of the work place, and Joint Shop Steward Committees are increasingly given 'official' recognition by both management and unions. But in a multi-site organisation this can only be the first step. Effective union influence here requires inter-union organisation *between* the various work places in the organisation.

 Do you ever have meetings with shop stewards from other work places in your organisation?

Are these meetings:

— with shop stewards from other work places that happen to be in the same region?

— with shop stewards from other work places in the same product group or division?

— with shop stewards from all work places within the organisation?

Reviewing existing organisation

Where links do exist between work places in the same organisation, these often grow out of regional comparisons of pay levels and

WE NEED TO FIND OUT WHAT IS HAPPENING IN THE SCOTTISH PLANT

conditions. Links are made with the work places that are nearest. But as we have seen, the structure of large organisations is often based on product groups or divisions, which may have within them sites in all corners of the country. While a locally or regionally co-ordinated trade union approach may be very effective on questions of wages and basic conditions, when it comes to influencing for example future manpower requirements for a particular product group or division, existing forms of inter-site co-operation may need reviewing. New contacts may have to be made with shop stewards in quite different parts of the country who are part of the same product group or division.

Public Sector

Public service unions are facing a similar need to review their forms of inter-union co-operation. For example, if unions want to influence the allocation of resources within local authorities as a whole then unions need joint organisation above the level of individual departments. The National Local Government Committee of NALGO has recommended that there should be a Workers Council in every local authority composed of elected representatives of all recognised trade unions. The establishment of such a council would

'ensure that a common trade union viewpoint is expressed regarding the policies and conduct of local authorities rather than a narrow departmental approach.'
NALGO 'Industrial Democracy' 1977.

In nationalised industries, company-wide links already exist between trade unions. For here *industry level* bargaining coincides with *company level* bargaining, and company level trade union machinery already exists in the form of the union side of the various Joint National Councils. The problem here is that most JNCs are composed of full-time officers only and so provide little help in improving communication between shop stewards at company level. An important issue for shop stewards in nationalised industries is likely to be the provision for lay representation on company level trade union machinery. British Airways provides an interesting example of moves in this direction. The trade union side of the National Joint Council for Civil Air Transport have recently agreed to the establishment of a British Airways Trade Union Council comprising the 28 members of the Trade Union Side of the NJC and 38 shop stewards and staff representatives. The proposed terms of reference for the Council are —

'to be responsible for the Joint Trade Union view (outside of the current negotiating structure on terms and conditions of employment) on matters relating to the operation and planning of British Airways and for the determination of Worker Participation in British Airways Management'.

Private Sector

In some private companies — chiefly American firms such as Ford that have not joined industry-wide employers organisations — management have encouraged company level bargaining which means that trade unions have had to develop their own company-level union organisation. But once again the union representatives are usually full time officials, and indeed it is often management's aim to limit shop stewards' power and influence.

However, in Ford, strong pressure from shop stewards has resulted in lay representation on the National Joint Negotiating Committee. Four convenors were elected to the NJNC after the 1969 Ford strike.

In the vast majority of large companies in the private sector, as the TUC has pointed out, there is a big gap between local bargaining machinery and industry-level bargaining machinery:

'on the one hand local and plant bargaining do not affect planning and investment decisions and, on the other, national agreements are not concerned with the management decisions of individual firms'.
Industrial Democracy, TUC 1974.

It is to fill this gap that in a number of companies shop stewards have formed their own company-wide combine committees. There is a WEA booklet on *'Multi-Plant Working and Trade Union Organisation'* which contains a great deal of valuable information about how existing combines developed and sets out the steps involved in setting up a combine from scratch. As the booklet explains, most combines have evolved slowly over a number of years starting with correspondence between plant shop stewards committees on questions like inter-plant comparisons of wages and working conditions and progressing to more formal organisation with regular meetings, officers, constitutions and so on.

Companies where combine committees exist include British Leyland, Ford, Lucas Aerospace, Shell, Vickers, Chrysler and Dunlop-Pirelli. Details of the experience of some of these combines can be found in the WEA booklet.

Many of these combines developed as a direct response to the increasing size of organisations, often associated with mergers. For example, the 'trigger' for the British Leyland combine was the merger of BMC and Leyland to form British Leyland, and the formation of the Lucas Aerospace combine was very much a response to the acquisition by Lucas of parts of English Electric.

An effective combine requires sound financial support and a carefully thought-out constitution which ensures strong links with plant shop stewards committees and the wider membership.

The Lucas combine provides in its constitution that the combine shall be financed by an affiliation fee of 10p per member per annum. Most combines have constitutions setting out questions like the system of plant representation, the frequency of meetings, the election of officers, the procedures for plants putting items on a combine meeting agenda, and the circulation of agendas and minutes to all plants.

The Ford combine established an Annual Delegate Conference open to all shop stewards of the company in order to prevent the combine from developing into an elite of shop stewards isolated from the rest. The Lucas combine tries to make combine meetings as open as possible by providing that each plant shop stewards committee may send as many representatives as they want to combine meetings as long as they meet their expenses. Actual voting however is constitutionally limited to one vote per site.

Some combines have established newspapers to improve communications and information-flow with the wider membership in the company. The British Leyland combine produces 'The Clarion' and the Lucas combine produces 'Combine News'. These papers report on combine meetings, on developments in particular plants, and on overall company plans.

If a combine is to be fully representative of all workers in a company, then staff representation is an important issue. Some combines are based solely on manual workers. The Lucas Combine however represents all Lucas Aerospace workers from the semi-skilled to the highest level technologists. This co-operation is important not only in terms of general solidarity, but also in terms of ensuring that all the knowledge and expertise concentrated in a highly skilled work force can be used to back up trade union organisation and policy-making. The Lucas Combine already operates its own Pensions Advisory Service, Health and Safety Committee, and Technology Advisory Service (which provides information and advice about the difficulties likely to be associated within the introduction of a new technology or process) and has recently drawn on all the expertise within the work force to draw up its own corporate plan putting forward proposals for product diversification which will safeguard members jobs in the future. (This plan is illustrated and explained in the TU Studies Year 2 programme 'The Right to Work'; how its ideas are being applied in other industries is also discussed in the film by spokesmen from the combines of Chrysler and Vickers.)

Combines and official trade union machinery

A major problem for all combines has been to secure the official blessing of unions and full time officers. The WEA booklet records that in its early days the British Leyland combine 'had the official blessing of all the unions concerned with the thirteen trade union officials attending its first meeting'. As the minutes of one of the early combine meetings put it: 'The aim of the committee would be to work within the framework of the Trade Union organisation and never to supercede it or be in conflict with it'.

In practice this was to prove difficult.

 What do you think are the problems raised for individual unions by the development of combine committees?

One problem relates to the separate democratic policy making machinery of different unions. It is difficult for trade union officials to support policies and strategies decided on in bodies with delegates from many different unions. But ways have been found of coping with this problem in relation to plant level joint shop stewards committees. The need is for this experience to be extended to company level combines.

Do you have a joint shop steward committee at your work place? Is it given official recognition or support by the various unions involved?

The position of full-time officers

The development of joint shop steward organisation can make full-time officers feel that their authority and negotiating functions are taken over by shop stewards. This raises the whole question of what the relationship between full-time officers and shop stewards should be.

The NUPE re-organisation we discussed earlier was based on the view that the important role for full-time officers in the future is one of support and advice to lay committees.

A similar view was expressed by Moss Evans during the 1969 Ford strike:

'I think the national negotiating body should be convenors — with the national officers along in an advisory capacity, to represent the official union . . . We ought to be there to offer some help to the lay people if they need it. Nothing more.'
Quoted in 'Working for Ford' Huw Beynon, Penguin, 1973

The AUEW has argued that the current Ford approach of a national negotiating committee with both full-time official and shop steward representation provides

'a sensible approach to constitutionalising Combine Committees, which, it has to be admitted, have in the main operated at best on a semi-official basis. The NJNCs of companies such as Vauxhalls and Fords provide a vital link between officials, stewards and members which is missing in combine committees, and results in our members not receiving the service they need.'
An investigation into the Scope of Industrial Democracy, AUEW, 1976

What do you think is the best relationship between full-time officers and shop stewards organisations?

Development in union policy

There is evidence that unions are becoming increasingly aware of the importance of supporting the establishment of combine committees and ensuring that such committees have effective links with official trade union machinery. For example, AUEW TASS has supported the establishment of combines since the following motion was passed at its 1970 Annual Conference:

'. . . Conference believes that the time has arrived to set up combine committees, such combine committees to consist of representatives from each establishment within a group. The Committee to appoint its own secretary and chairman and arrange its own meetings to which appropriate Executive Committee and Divisional organisers would be invited.'

The 1974 and 1975 Annual Conferences decided to appoint convening officials for each combine with responsibility for the production of monthly reports and regular bulletins for circulation through the Combine, and above all responsibility for the convening of Delegates Conferences for each Combine.

Has your union conference ever discussed the development of combine organisation?

Most unions are only prepared as yet to tackle the question of company level organisation on an individual union basis. But if all unions actively supported such developments, there would be an official basis for inter-union co-operation at company level. For example APEX have set up a National Negotiating Committee of APEX representatives within the Lucas Electrical Division. 47 locations of Lucas Electrical can each send a representative to the National Group Meeting which meets about 6 times a year. The group meeting elects 8 shop stewards and 4 officers to form the national negotiating committee. A national officer of APEX is also a member of the national negotiating committee, which meets as often as required. The union has assigned research officers to the NNC for specific issues like job evaluation and maternity leave.

TUC policy
What is the TUC attitude to all this?

In its 1977 Economic Review the TUC argues that the establishment of company level trade union organisation is essential for the success of the industrial strategy and for the extension of industrial democracy:

'The establishment of effective company-level machinery which does not undermine either existing machinery or the policy-making procedures of particular unions is clearly a complex matter which requires detailed consideration. But it is a question to which both the TUC and affiliated unions must devote substantial time and resources in the coming year'.

Forming combine committees
A practical guide on how to go about setting up a combine committee has been drawn up by the Tyne Conference of Shop Stewards Working Party and is reproduced in the WEA booklet on 'Multi-Plant Working and Trade Union Organisation'. It gives valuable advice for any group of workers trying to develop company level trade union organisation, under four main headings (obtainable from WEA, 9 Upper Berkeley Street, London W1H 8BY):

1 Who is your employer.
2 Where are your employers plants.
3 What is your company doing.
4 Contact with other workers.

Under each of these headings the guide suggests sources of information, either through reference books, union facilities, or informal contacts. For groups of trade unionists seeking information on any of these questions it would be of great assistance.

STUDIES
FOR
TRADE
UNIONISTS

MULTI-PLANT WORKING
and
TRADE UNION ORGANISATION
by
HENRY FRIEDMAN

Coping with a large organisation (4)

Establishing joint union-management machinery at key levels of the company

Company-wide trade union organisation is essential for shop stewards to co-ordinate their strategies and policies. But strategies are useless unless they can be implemented and implementation usually requires bargaining with management. The establishment of recognised joint negotiating machinery at company level is not likely to be achieved without a struggle. This final section reviews some of the progress that is being made.

In the last section we looked at the example of APEX setting up company level trade union machinery which has achieved recognition from management for bargaining on certain company level issues.

Joint shop stewards combine committees however have often experienced much greater problems in getting management recognition to bargain. The experience of the Lucas Aerospace combine provides a good illustration of this.

At first management was willing to meet the combine informally to discuss certain issues. But when the combine began to take up a clear negotiating stance—particularly in relation to the combine's corportate plan for product diversification to safeguard jobs—management refused to enter into company level negotiations. They would only agree to site by site talks through 'local consultative machinery'. Soon afterwards management wrote a formal letter to the combine committee making it clear that they did not recognise the body. This re-exposed a critical weakness in the position of the combine—that the status of the committee and its relation to the unions' official machinery had not been properly sorted out.

One key question raised by this example is whether workers in multi-plant organisations are prepared to use sanctions to get management recognition for combine committees. It is also a powerful reminder of the point made in chapter 1 that the recognition issue is still a live one.

 Do you think your members would be prepared to take industrial action to get management recognition for a combine committee?

Consultation or negotiation?

Most employers are strongly defensive of their 'prerogatives' in relation to company planning. They tend to want to restrict union involvement in company-level decision making to consultation only.

As we saw in the first chapter, consultation often means in management terms just informing workers about what decisions management have taken, and trying to get union representatives to sell these to their members.

Most of the highly-publicised participation schemes put forward by management recently are purely consultative in nature. British Leyland is one such example. The participation scheme involves three levels of joint committees—the lowest at plant level, the second at divisional level, and a top level Council. Clear lines of demarcation are established between existing collective bargaining arrangements and the new participation structure. The committees give shop stewards access to the relevant levels of management to discuss a wide range of issues including product plans, capital allocation and the development and reviewing of budgets at each level. The limitation of these committees from the union point of view is that their objective is 'to seek as far as possible to reach agreement on action required while recognising that executive responsibility rests with management'. In other words, if agreement can't be reached, management is free to go ahead unilaterally.

The Leyland Combine Committee has been split, and as a result considerably weakened, over the issue of union involvement in this participation scheme.

Do you think unions should press for nothing short of negotiation on all aspects of company policy?

Is there a case for arguing that consultation can be a transitional stage towards negotiation?

Another participation scheme, this time in Harland and Wolff, provides an example of how one group of trade unionists have tried to bridge this gap between consultation and negotiation.

The Harland and Wolff unions have agreed to a three-tier structure similar to that at British Leyland with a Joint Implementation Council at the top, and Joint Departmental Councils and Productivity Committees beneath.

While the Harland and Wolff committees are once more essentially consultative and not negotiating bodies, there is a very important clause in the agreement specifying that 'failure to reach agreement at the JIC means the use of collective bargaining structures'. In other words, management would not be free as at Leyland to go ahead despite union objections; any policy issue on which agreement could not be reached would effectively become a collective bargaining issue. It could be that this scheme could act as a catalyst to the extension of collective bargaining to many aspects of company policy-making. Only experience will tell.

Action checklist
● Do some research on the structure, and where relevant, ownership of your organisation.
Draw up a diagram showing how your work place relates to other levels of the organisation, and discuss this with your fellow shop stewards.
● Make sure you are fully informed about the management structure in your organisation and about who has the power to make what decisions.
● Discuss the measures you could take to improve union organisation within your organisation as a whole, for example:
— exchanging information/organising meeting with shop stewards at other work places belonging to the organisation.
— discussion with full time officers on how to develop or make more effective trade union machinery at a company level.
— putting forward a resolution to your branch urging your union to take practical steps to support the development of combines.
— putting forward a resolution to your branch urging your union to review its structure and organisation in the light of new demands posed by the growth of large organisations.
● Work out what sort of joint union-management machinery at company level would best fit the structure of your organisation and the aims of trade unionists within it.

Chapter 7   Workers On The Board?

We have seen in previous chapters that in order to win any effective control over many important aspects of their working lives, trade unionists need to have a say in top-level planning decisions within their employing organisations. We have also seen some of the difficulties met by unions trying to establish a right to bargain on such forward planning issues. Many managers still see planning decisions as their 'prerogative'. They may 'consult' with workers' representatives on some issues — but the final decision usually remain their alone. Given this situation, the idea of workers having a legal right to ask for representation on the very bodies that take these important planning decisions has certain attractions. At the same time many trade unionists have strong reservations about such a development.

The concern of this chapter is to look more closely at some of the 'pros' and 'cons' of board representation, in order to help you clarify your own views on this important issue. (This chapter is focused mainly on the private sector, leaving the public sector situation to the next chapter).

Questions
Note down your answers to these questions before watching the television programme or working through the chapter.

Yes No

1 Have you personally ever been involved in debates on the question of worker representation on company boards:

☐ ☐ at your workplace

☐ ☐ at your branch

☐ ☐ at your union conference

2 What is your view at present on this question?

☐ in favour of board representation

☐ opposed to board representation

☐ undecided

3 What do you see as the main attractions of board representation?
. . . .
. . . .

4 What do you see as the main problems raised by board representation for unions? . . . .
. . . .

Yes No

☐ ☐ **5** Does your union have a national policy on board representation?

6 Which of these two statements do you agree with most:

☐ 'Board representation would strengthen the collective bargaining position of the unions'

☐ 'Board representation would weaken the collective bargaining position of unions'

7 Would the fact of whether a firm was in public or private ownership make any difference to your attitude to board representation?

☐   ☐

8 At the present time does collective bargaining in your company cover:

☐   ☐   investment decisions

☐   ☐   product decisions

☐   ☐   pricing policy

☐   ☐   location of new factories

☐   ☐   mergers

9 Do you think it is possible to establish bargaining on all of these issues?

☐   ☐

Issues for the chapter

After working through the chapter you should have a clearer idea of:

1 The potential benefits of board representation

2 the potential problems of board representation

3 the arguments put forward for and against within the trade union movement

4 what British unions can learn from European experience.

The debate within the unions

Here, in a very simplified way, are some of the main arguments put forward for and against worker representation on boards —

For
1 Makes private companies accountable to workers as well as shareholders.
2 Eats into 'owner prerogatives'.
3 Gives better access to management information especially at top levels of decision making.
4 Allows for positive trade union initiatives at a stage when decisions can really be influenced.

Extends collective bargaining to the boardroom.

Against
1 Means trade unions are committed to promoting private profit.
2 Forces trade unions to accept joint responsibility for management decisions.
3 Mixes up the trade union and management functions and weakens union independence.
4 Puts trade unions under conflicting pressures from their members and the company.

Weakens union ability to oppose management through collective bargaining.

Now lets look in more detail at what is involved in these arguments.

The arguments for board representation

Making companies accountable to workers as well as shareholders
At present companies are accountable in law only to their shareholders.

When managers talk about the 'best interests of the company' this means in strict legal terms 'the interests of the shareholders'. In the eyes of the law, the company *is* the shareholders.

But trade unions have long argued that shareholders are not the only group who 'invest' in a company and therefore have an interest in its management. After all, workers invest their livelihood in a company. This is what the TUC General Secretary has said on this point:

'The interest of the workers in the well-being of their company is surely as great, if not greater, than that of the shareholder, and anything a company achieves is achieved by a partnership of the two main factors of production, capital and labour. It is high time that we moved towards a form of industrial organisation that recognised capital and labour as equal partners'.

The TUC have argued that company law should be changed to place on companies a *legal obligation* to have regard to the interests of work people as well as shareholders, and indeed many managers would also support this change. Where the TUC goes further than management is in demanding that workers should have *equal rights* with shareholders in terms of *representation* on company boards. This would give workers the power to make sure that company decisions reflect their interests as well as shareholder interests.

Getting-in on the top-level decisions

We saw in the last chapter that workers employed in a subsidiary of a large group often don't even know what decisions are being *considered* at holding company level; and when they do it is usually too late to influence the decision. If workers had a right to board representation at both subsidiary and holding company level, they could be involved in decisions right from the beginning and have full access to all the information.

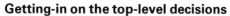 Can you think of instances in your company when by the time you heard about a particular management decision it was too late to influence it in any way?

Limits to collective bargaining

Some of those in favour of board representation argue that while it is important to extend collective bargaining as far as possible, there are some issues that can never really be dealt with through bargaining. This is what the TUC said in their 1974 statement on 'Industrial Democracy':

'Major decisions on investment, location, closures, takeovers and mergers, and product specialisation of the organisation are generally taken at levels where collective bargaining does not take place, and indeed are subject matter not readily covered by collective bargaining. New forms of control are needed'.

In their evidence to the Bullock Committee of Inquiry on Industrial Democracy, APEX gave some examples of 'issues that are not amenable to resolution by existing negotiating procedures'. They listed four main issues:

A merger with another company
Establishment of companies overseas
Establishment of new factories within the U.K.
Full disclosure of information

On the question of mergers, APEX comments that 'the only people who can control a merger between two companies ultimately are the shareholders of both companies under present law. It is not possible to conceive of an extension of negotiations between unions and employers that will give unions a veto over such matters'. Board representation could however provide such a veto power. In other words, it could eat into 'owner prerogatives' as well as 'management prerogatives'.

On the question of disclosure of information, APEX points out that 'the requirements of the Industry Act on Planning Agreements and the requirements of the Employment Protection Act both limit information that can be made available to trade unions because of secrecy requirements and the competitive needs of companies'. There are no such limitations on the other hand on the information that can be made available to board members.

From your own experience can you think of any other issues which unions might be able to influence more effectively through board representation than through collective bargaining?

Who appoints management?
One important issue that might have occurred to you is the appointment of management. It is hard to see how workers could ever achieve this through conventional bargaining.

Plant closure
Conventional methods have not always been adequate for dealing with threatened closures. Typically workers get no information at all until the decision is well advanced and redundancy notices are being issued. In this situation, it is hard for unions to have any real influence on the decision. They are usually forced into bargaining about the *terms* of redundancy — not about whether the factory should close at all. This has led workers to experiment with new forms of action like the sit-in and work-in. But even these new forms of action have been limited in their success:

'Sit-ins have . . . often been a last desperate act of a work force that has apparently reached the end of the line, and is unable to influence a decision taken elsewhere . . . The need for this form of defensive industrial action indicates the kinds of decisions that remain outside the collective bargaining process and this pinpoints the limitation of collective bargaining'.
TUC 'Industrial Democracy'

Positive Action by Unions
It has been argued that if workers were represented on boards, they would know well in advance that the closure of a particular factory or a reduction in its work force was an option under consideration. They would be in a position to put forward *positive alternatives* in terms of new product or new marketing strategy which might safeguard job security. Trade unions could move from a defensive role to a positive role. If workers had 50% representation on the board they would be in a position to exert real influence and where there was disagreement, management would have to be prepared to 'bargain' to reach agreement. In other words the practical effect of worker representation on boards would be *to extend collective bargaining into the boardroom.*

UCS workers lobby Parliament about proposed closure of their yard 1971

Union doubts

In 1974 the Trades Union Congress passed the resolution urging that:

'any extension of trade union participation in industrial management shall be, and be seen to be, an extension of collective bargaining, and shall in no sense compromise the unions role as here defined'.

Some trade unionists have argued that to press for board representation in no way conflicts with this resolution, as long as the representation is through trade union machinery on a 50/50 basis. Others see this resolution as a rejection of board representation, because they feel that trade union involvement at board level would inevitably compromise the unions' traditional collective bargaining role.

Mixing up the union and management functions

Collective bargaining, it is argued, involves two separate groups with quite distinct functions — it is management's job to take the decisions and the union's job to oppose these decisions where they threaten members' interests. Management is responsible for the viability of the company as a whole, but the unions are responsible only to their membership.

Board representation, it is argued, *mixes up* these separate functions. Trade union representatives on the board would have to take account of the interests of the company as a whole and not just of the interests of their membership. The danger is that workers would become absorbed into management, even if they had equal representation, because all boards do is rubber stamp decisions reached by management experts outside the boardroom.

To make things worse, although they had no real influence over decisions, worker representatives would be forced to accept *responsibility* for board decisions, and this would limit their power to oppose these decisions later on through collective bargaining.

The EEPTU is a union that has argued strongly against worker representation on boards. Here are some extracts from their evidence to the Bullock Committee:

'. . . it is essential that trade unions retain their independence. It will be difficult for trade union directors to accept responsibility for managerial decisions and represent the workers who feel they must oppose them . . . Far better in the interests of those affected by a managerial decision that the responsibility for that decision is firmly laid at the management's door; then the collective bargaining machinery can oppose and moderate the impact of the decision when necessary.'

This quotation implies that it must always be the union's job to *react* to decisions after they are made by management. Unions seek to exercise a kind of veto power over management decisions.

What in your opinion is the objective of industrial democracy? Giving unions extended veto powers over management decision, or making policy-making a joint process where workers are involved just as much as management?

(You might like to look back at Chapter 1 pp 15-16 where this issue was briefly discussed).

AMALGAMATED UNION OF ENGINEERING WORKERS

**An Investigation
into the Scope of
Industrial Democracy**

June, 1976

The Profit Motive

Other arguments against board representation have been concerned more with the question of the ownership and objectives of companies. Privately owned companies it is argued are concerned to make as much profit as possible, sometimes through rationalisation that may be against the interests of the workers, at least in the short term. If trade unionists were represented on the boards of such companies, they would have to accept responsibility for objectives dominated by maximising profit and shareholders' dividends. The AUEW policy statement 'An Investigation into the scope of Industrial Democracy' makes a distinction between 'the private sector being run purely for profit and the public sector which should be run in the interests of the public'; board representation is supported *only* in publicly owned companies.

At the 1976 Trade Union Congress John Forrester of TASS argued that 'The role of the trade union movement in a private enterprise concern must be different from the role of the trade union movement in a publicly owned concern.'

Do you agree that the objectives of publicly owned industries are fundamentally different from the objectives of private companies, and does this mean a different role for trade unions?

Keeping the options open

Some trade unions are not fundamentally opposed to the concept of board representation. But they take the view that the extension of collective bargaining machinery will be the immediate concern of most groups of workers. In their evidence to the Bullock Committee the GMWU argued that:

'The *option* of a supervisory board should be included in company law . . . In some cases it may be desirable but in most cases — at least immediately — other forms of machinery will be devised.'

TUC policy has always stressed that board representation should not be imposed on trade unions. It should be a legal right available to organised workers who choose to use it.

Learning from experience

How often have you heard people say 'Board representation doesn't work — you only have to look at British Steel (or Germany)'. How valid are such generalisations? Unfortunately they provide no simple answers, chiefly because board representation can take many different forms. But by looking at the different forms of board representation that have been tried we can certainly get a clearer idea of what forms of board representation *don't* work and highlight some of the pitfalls to be avoided.

U.K. experience — British Steel Corporation

The only major union-backed experiment in board representation in this country so far has been in British Steel. The British Steel experiment is described in the TUC document Industrial Democracy. In brief it involved the appointment of worker directors to the divisional boards of BSC. But the worker directors were *not* elected by the workers; they were appointed by the BSC from a short-list presented by the TUC Steel Committee. Originally on appointment the worker directors had to give up trade union office, although since 1972 this ruling has been dropped.

113

There is general agreement that the experiment was not successful in its early form for two main reasons:

1 worker directors were not elected representatives of the workforce.

2 the links with trade union machinery were weak.

Moreover, the boards, on which the worker directors sit are *not* policy-making boards but advisory boards only.
A full account of how the scheme has been improved is given by the BSC worker-directors themselves in 'Worker Directors Speak' (paperback obtainable from Gower Press, Westmead, Farnborough, Hants.).

The lessons of the BSC experiment would seem to be that for board representation to have any chance of being effective, it must take place on a board with real policy-making powers, and representatives must be elected by and accountable to the work force through trade union machinery. European experience points in a similar direction.

European experience
France, Germany, Holland, Norway, Denmark and Sweden all have some form of worker representation on boards. The EEC has also issued a '5th directive' and a green paper on the harmonisation of board representation provision in common market countries. This section concentrates on Germany, Sweden and Italy as three contrasting case studies of different union strategies.

Germany — Legal provision
It is Germany that has had the longest experience of worker representation on boards. There are now three systems of board representation in operation, all of which involve a two tier system. Workers are represented on a *supervisory board* which then elects a *management board*. It is the management board that makes policy, but decisions of the board on certain specified issues have to go to the supervisory board for approval.

Since the Codetermination Act of 1951 there has been a form of 'parity' representation in coal and steel. Out of an 11 man board, five are elected by the workers, five by the shareholders, with an eleventh member jointly co-opted by both sides as an 'independent chairman'. Of the five worker representatives, two are nominated by the works council, two by the trade unions, and one is nominated by the German Trade Union Federation to represent the 'public interest':

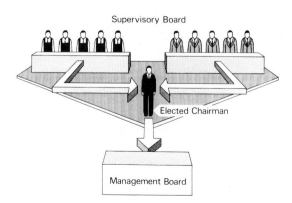

Supervisory Board

Elected Chairman

Management Board

Since the Works Constitution Act of 1952 all other joint stock companies with over 500 employees have a system of *minority* worker representation at board level. One third of the board are elected by a ballot of all employees. There is no special provision for trade union representation:

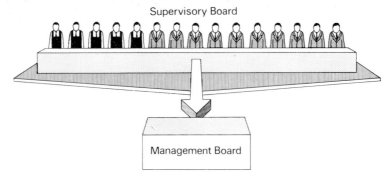

It has been an objective of the German trade unions to extend parity representation to the whole of industry. Following pressure from the trade unions, a new Codetermination Act was passed in 1976 establishing 'parity representation' in all companies employing over 2,000 workers. The trade unions are not happy with the new Act since it contains provisions which, in their view, ensure that worker representatives will be in a permanent minority still. For the Act stipulates that if there is disagreement over the appointment of the chairman (who has a casting vote) the ultimate right of appointment should lie with the shareholders; furthermore there is provision that the worker representative group must always have within it as *least one representative of 'senior management'*.

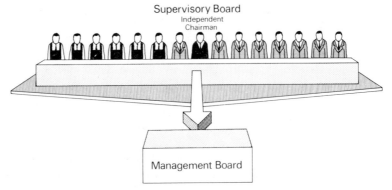

So while the German unions are committed to parity representation at board level, they have still not achieved it except in coal and steel, and even here it can be argued that the role of the independent chairman prevents a true parity situation. Moreover, German law still gives the general meeting of shareholders the ultimate right to veto board decisions, so even with parity the shareholders would still have the upper hand.

The lessons
So what does German experience tell us about the operation and effectiveness of board representation?
One interesting point is that experience suggests that parity representation *does* give rise to something akin to negotiation in the boardroom.

On the question of how effective worker directors are in influencing policy decisions, the research evidence is rather negative. Worker representatives appear to have had little impact upon the nature of companies decisions on questions like investment, dividends, take-over and rationalisation. What they seem to have concentrated on is the agreement of adequate 'social plans' to protect workers as far as possible against the adverse *consequences* of these decisions.

A number of reasons have been put forward to explain this lack of impact:

1 policy is made on the management board and its sub-committees on which workers are not represented; the supervisory board merely 'reacts' to these decisions.

2 worker representatives are under strong social pressures to behave like 'proper directors'.

3 legally the worker representatives are required to behave in the manner of 'an orderly and conscientious business manager'.

4 the legal requirements of confidentiality prevent full accountability to the workforce.

5 links with unions that might give worker representatives some independence from management are weak in the German system.

6 any influence worker representatives can have is limited by market considerations of competitive position etc.

Sweden

Since 1973 there has been a law in Sweden giving workers in firms employing over 100 people the right to appoint two representatives to the board. It is up to the unions to decide whether or not to exercise this right and representatives are elected through trade union machinery. Representation takes place on the existing board, which is a one-tier or unitary board, on the lines of existing UK company boards:

Management Board

From the union point of view the Swedish system is clearly an improvement in many respects on the German system. Representation is firmly based on union machinery and only goes ahead where unions request it. So where workers are poorly organised they are unlikely to opt for board representation. In 82% of the firms covered by the Act, unions have taken up their right to board representation.

The fact that workers are in a minority on the board was not something forced on the unions; it was a conscious choice. The strategy of Swedish unions has been to see board representation as a means of *getting information* rather than actually influencing decisions. The information gained at board level can then be used to influence decisions through collective bargaining —

'Access to information with regard to long-term planning would enable the trade union organisations to initiate discussion within the works council

and other bodies such as the safety committee or in project groups at an early enough stage to influence subsequent planning and decisions.'
'Industrial Democracy: Programme adopted by the 1971 Congress of the Swedish Trade Union Confederation.

By stopping short at minority representation, Swedish unions hope to avoid some of the problems of pressure to take joint responsibility for board decisions that tends to go with parity representation.

How well has this strategy of gaining information worked for the unions?

A report by the National Swedish Industrial Board found that at least half the worker representatives on boards were dissatisfied with the information they received. Much of the information given to worker representatives was felt to be incomplete, and was not distributed until late, sometimes not until the meeting itself. Nevertheless there was no indication that shareholder representatives received any better information. Another problem for unions was that they were not represented on sub-committees of the board where much of the most important information was discussed. This has subsequently been rectified by new legislation.

On the whole the Swedish unions seem satisfied that board representation performs a useful function as a back-up to more traditional union methods.

Italy

Italy provides an example of yet another union strategy. As a CIR report has commented:

'The subjects of worker directors and alternative forms of direct employee participation in management attract little support and only a limited level of discussion in Italy. The unions view such concepts with considerable suspicion as being calculated to dilute the impact of unions on management and involving an inherent conflict of roles in the position of the worker director. Union strategy has been to place primary importance on maintenance of pressure on employers through the process of collective bargaining'.

Italian unions have had limited success in establishing bargaining on issues like the location of new plants within Italy. One example was the success of Fiat workers in forcing management to relieve unemployment by building a new plant in the depressed south.

Has this brief review of some European experience made you modify your views on board representation in any way?

Before judging the British Steel experience of worker directors, you would need to examine what they themselves say about it in the paperback mentioned above.

Two approaches to board representation

European experience reflects the same division of views between unions as there are in Britain. Even when unions favour board representation they may still adopt one of two very different strategies:

1 board representation as a form of joint decision making — parity representation. (Extending collective bargaining to the board room).

2 board representation as a source of information to strengthen collective bargaining procedures — minority representation.

117

To be effective, research suggests that either system needs to be based on trade union machinery, and workers need to be represented on a board where real policy discussions take place.

Worker representatives are better placed to influence decisions if there is a degree of planning in the economy as a whole, involving both unions and government.

TUC policy

TUC policy on board representation is contained in the document 'Industrial Democracy' adopted by the 1974 Congress. It is important reading for all trade unionists. The main points of TUC policy can be summarised as follows:

1 equal representation for workers and shareholders.

2 worker representatives to be elected through trade union machinery.

3 representation to take place on a board with real policy-making powers, and powers to overrule the AGM of shareholders.

4 trade unions would be free to decide whether or not to take up their right to representation.

In its emphasis on the central role of trade unions, TUC policy is very similar to the Swedish approach. But in contrast to the Swedish unions' policy of minority representation only as a source of information, the TUC approach has been to see board representation as a means of extending joint decision-making to the board room.

Joint responsibility for joint decisions?

In the 1974 policy document the TUC argued that a system of board representation must be devised that 'leaves the lines of responsibility of the workers' representatives to their constituents . . . It is no use requiring that worker-directors should behave just like any other directors.'

But in their supplementary evidence to the Bullock committee, (printed in the 1977 edition of Industrial Democracy) the TUC made it clear that in return for equal representation worker representatives on the board should accept equal responsibility with shareholder representatives for board decisions and the general interests of the enterprise. In other words, worker representatives on the board would have a 'dual responsibility to workers and the enterprise'.

 As a trade unionist would you find it possible to accept this dual responsibility?

It might be argued that in all negotiations trade unionists have to consider the interests of the enterprise as well as the interests of the members, because the jobs of their members depend on the viability of the enterprise. What is your view on this?

It might also be argued that even with minority representation, worker representatives on the board would still be under pressure to accept full responsibility for board decisions, without having any real influence on these decisions. At least with equal representation workers have some chance of influencing decisions for which they will be held responsible. In their supplementary evidence to Bullock the TUC explains that 'The TUC advocates parity trade union shareholder representation at board level in order to avoid a situation of trade union representatives being given responsibility without a real share in decision making'.

 What are your views on this question?

The problems of achieving parity

In looking at German experience we saw that the trade union objective of parity in the boardroom is not easily achieved. Employers and governments have always tried to keep workers in the minority.

In Britain the Bullock report recommended equal representation for workers and shareholders (as a way of ensuring that workers would accept equal responsibility for board decisions). But the kind of equal representation advocated is very different from the 50/50 proposal originally put forward by the TUC. In addition to equal numbers of workers and shareholder representatives, there would be a smaller group of jointly agreed 'independent' members on the board. $(2x + y$ formula):

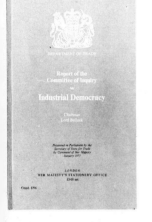

Management Board

Elected

We saw earlier that one reason for trade unions favouring parity representation was that it offered a means of extending collective bargaining to the board room.

 How do you think the Bullock proposals affect the achievement of this objective?

You might find it helpful in making up your mind to think about the following comment from a TUC document on the Bullock report, circulated for discussion to affiliated unions:

'Since the third group of directors would be jointly agreed, it can be argued that the principle of equal representation, which is the key to TUC policy, is safeguarded. At the same time, however, trade unionists are bound to have certain doubts about how the $2x + y$ formula would work in practice . . . The advantage of a 50/50 form of equal representation is that the trade union side could not be outvoted — agreement would have to be reached by compromise and negotiation. In a $2x + y$ situation there will inevitably be fears that many 'independents' would take the management point of view in a conflict situation.'
Industrial Democracy: The Next Steps

At the same time the TUC document implies that it would be 'politically unlikely' to achieve straight 50/50 representation without any form of independent chairman.

What attitude do you think the unions should take on this issue?

The Bullock report argues that the presence of a third group of directors will 'reduce the tendency found in Germany in coal and steel for employees and shareholder representatives to vote and act as distinct groups'.

 What do you think of this argument?

One-tier or two-tier boards

Debates about board representation often lead into some very complicated and technical discussions about the structure of company boards. We saw that in Germany worker representation on boards takes place within a two-tier board structure, workers being represented on a supervisory board which oversees the work of a management board. There are no actual managers sitting on the supervisory board. In German law no person can be a member of *both* boards. In Sweden on the other hand workers were represented on a one-tier or unitary board, very much like the existing board structure of British companies. The shareholder representatives on this board would normally be managers of the company.

What if anything do these differences of approach mean for trade unionists? To some extent, how many tiers a board has is irrelevant. The important question for trade unionists is *what powers* lie with the board on which worker representatives sit. A good example of how the power of boards can vary is offered by the majority and minority reports of the Bullock Committee. The majority report recommends worker representation on a one-tier board which would have reserved to it by law certain key policy making powers which could not be delegated to management. The minority report, signed by employer representatives, recommends employee representation on a supervisory board which would have no powers of initiative on policy-making.

In its 1974 document, the TUC argued for supervisory boards. But in its supplementary evidence to Bullock it recognised that there might be certain points in favour of worker representation on existing unitary boards in British companies.

Here are some of the advantages and disadvantages of one and two tier boards, in order to help you make up your mind on this issue —

Supervisory boards

Advantages

Trade union representatives on the supervisory board are clearly separated from management who sit on the management board. There is less danger of worker representatives being 'absorbed' into management and losing their independence.

Disadvantages

The real decisions tend to be made by the management board on which workers are not represented. The supervisory board usually has only veto powers over decisions already made and no powers to initiate policy. Not all information available to the management board might be released to the supervisory board.

Unitary boards

Advantages	Disadvantages
Because the board is a policy-making board worker representatives are more likely to be involved in the real policy discussions and can take positive initiatives here.	Worker representatives will be sitting alongside professional managers. From their members' point of view, they may seem to be becoming part of the 'management structure' and losing their independence.

The issue for unions might be summarised as follows:

Do they stay independent of management and remain satisfied with limited and indirect influence. Or do they become more closely involved in the process of management policy-making at the risk of appearing to lose some of their independence?

 What are your views on this issue?

Collective bargaining and board representation

In thinking about the last question you may have remembered that we looked briefly at the dilemma of 'independence versus involvement' in the first chapter when we were discussing the extension of collective bargaining.

So can we really claim that if unions reject board representation and stick to collective bargaining, they avoid all the problems discussed in this chapter in relation to board representation?

Many of the union doubts about board representation relate to questions of how much joint responsibility unions should be prepared to shoulder, and how far there should be an overlapping of union and management functions. But we saw in the first chapter that unions *already* accept joint responsibility for collective agreements that may well be far from ideal. Moreover, as we saw, the whole process of extending industrial democracy has been about challenging the idea there there is a separate management function by insisting that more and more management decisions become the subject of joint decision making.

On the question of union independence, one danger in the boardroom situation is that workers may be under greater influence to 'see management's point of view' and accept management explanations, particularly on highly technical questions. But this can still happen in a collective bargaining situation.

 How often have you heard complaints that negotiators were 'brain-washed' by management?

In his 1976 speech to Congress, Len Murray argued that —

'the real safeguards . . . of trade union independence — both in the context of collective bargaining and in the context of board representation — will continue to be strong trade union organisation, responsive to and accountable to the membership. That must be backed up by effective trade union training, by research, by the provision of information which will help our representatives question management assumptions and develop their own alternative policies'.

(We return to this important question of training and industrial democracy in the last chapter).

 Having read this chapter and thinking back to some of the issues raised in chapter one, would you say that —

Board representation introduces fundamentally new problems for unions, or board representation highlights problems that unions will have to come to terms with anyway in their collective bargaining, if they are really committed to an extension of industrial democracy?

Trade Unions and Board Membership in Co-ops

Up to now we have been looking at the pros and cons of workers being represented along with shareholders on the boards of private companies. But what about the situation of a workers' co-operative where workers are the shareholders and will therefore be in a majority on the board? Does majority board membership and the fact that the company is run in the interests of its workers remove all the problems of trade union involvement in the boardroom that we have looked at so far?

At Meriden for example the board is made up of all eight shop stewards' convenors plus two part time advisers.

 Can you think of any problems that might arise for trade unionists where the majority of a board are shop stewards?

Some points on this:

1 Even if a firm is owned by workers, it still has to compete with other firms. Market pressures may force shop stewards in their role as directors to make cuts in the work force, or make demands for increased output without increased wages.

2 There could also be conflicts of loyalties arising from workers having a dual role as directors, who give management their instructions, and as shop stewards who negotiate with management about the effects of management actions on their members. This is what one commentator had to say on this question —

'Almost invariably the lead in launching a worker's co-op is taken by the shop stewards who find themselves playing a dual role once the co-op is in operation. Even a lay board of directors made up of militant trade unionists will inevitably identify itself with management.

. . . If the original trade union representatives are to continue as directors of the co-op then they should ensure that fresh shop stewards are trained to take their place so that union functions can be separated from management'.

Richard Fletcher 'Workers Co-ops and the Co-operative Movement' in 'The New Worker Cooperatives', Spokesman Books, 1976

This point is also relevant to worker representation on boards in private companies.

 Do you think there should be a separation of shop steward and worker director functions?

Or do you think it should be active shop stewards who are already involved in collective bargaining who represent the workers on the board?

Action checklist

● Discuss the question of board representation within your union branch and shop stewards committee in order to arrive if possible at an agreed policy (remember if there is legislation on the lines argued for by the TUC, the choice whether to go for representation on the board will be entirely up to the trade unions in each company).

● If you can see some possible advantages in board representation, draw up a list of powers and safeguards which would have to be built into a system of board representation before you as trade unionists were prepared to be involved in it.

● Discuss —

a how seats on the board would be allocated between various unions or groups of workers (Where there are a large number of unions it may not be possible for every union to be represented on the board).

b what new forms of union organisation might be needed below the board to back up and support board representation. e.g. a company level combine committee.

c the machinery through which worker representatives on the board would report back to the people they represent.

d whether worker directors should receive a fee, or just be paid for 'time-off' like normal shop stewards.

● If you are opposed to board representation, discuss what strategies you need to adopt in order to improve your access to management information and extend bargaining to long-term planning questions e.g.

the negotiation of information agreements with management
the agreement with management of company level bargaining procedures
the establishment of joint committees on say, investment or product plans.

Further reading

TUC 'Industrial Democracy', (January 1977 edition includes supplementary evidence to the Bullock Committee).
TUC Guide to the Bullock Report, 1977.
'Shop stewards Guide to the Bullock Report' Ken Coates and Tony Topham, Spokesman Books, 1977.
'What Kind of Industrial Democracy?' Mel Doyle, WEA Studies for Trade Unionists, Sept. 1976.
'Industrial Democracy: European Experience' Two reports prepared for the Industrial Democracy Committee by Eric Batstone and P L Davies, HMSO 1976.
'Worker Participation and Collective Bargaining in Europe', CIR Study No. 4 HMSO 1974.
'Workers Directors Speak', Gower Press paperback 1977 from Teakfield Ltd, Westmead, Farnborough, Hants. British Steel worker directors report their own experience in relation to the issues raised in this chapter.

Chapter 8   Servants of The Public?

Earlier we suggested that industrial democracy from the trade union viewpoint is about (i) reducing the sole control of management and (ii) bringing decisions by owners under trade union influence.

But what if the owners are the Government, or the public as taxpayers and ratepayers? Where this is the case management are accountable to democratically elected national or local representatives, who have the ultimate responsibility for policy matters. Does this mean that the union approach to industrial democracy has to be different in the public sector? Is there a potential clash here between *political* and industrial democracy? Does the fact that public service employees are theoretically 'servants of the public' mean they have to lower their sights in terms of industrial democracy? These are the questions we will explore in this chapter.

General questions
Note down your answers to these questions before working through the chapter or watching the television programme.

1 Do you work or have you ever worked for —
☐ a company where there is National Enterprise Board involvement
☐ a nationalised industry
☐ a public corporation
☐ a local authority
☐ the health service
☐ the civil service

Yes No
☐ ☐ Do you feel that your role there as a trade unionist was different to what it would be in a private firm?

2 In your view does the fact that a firm or service is in public ownership
☐ strengthen the case for trade union involvement in its management
☐ weaken the case for trade union involvement in its management
☐ make no difference at all to the case

☐ ☐ **3** Does your union have members in any public industries or services?

☐ ☐ Do you know what policies your union has put forward for extending industrial democracy in these areas?

☐ ☐ **4** Does your union have sponsored MPs in Parliament?

☐ ☐ **5** Are there any trade union representatives on your local council?

Issues for the chapter
After working through this chapter, you should have a clearer idea of:

1 who public industries and services are accountable to

2 the kinds of arguments put forward about the trade union role in publicly owned industries and services

3 some of the proposals put forward by unions for extending industrial democracy in these areas.

Comparing public and private sectors
Among those who accept the basic principles of trade unionism, there has been no real argument that all workers, wherever they are employed, have a basic right to bargain over the terms and conditions of their employment and over the implementation of management policies that affect these terms and conditions. In fact the Government as an employer has tended increasingly to see its role as one of establishing good practice in industrial relations by encouraging trade union membership and the development of collective bargaining. On average 83% of public sector workers are in trade unions as opposed to only 39% in the private sector. In this respect then, public ownership can be said to have had a positive effect on industrial democracy, as trade unionists see it. Where the debate starts is on the question of the extent of trade union involvement in actual *policy making* in the public sector.

In all parts of the public sector as the diagram shows, from NEB companies to local authorities, ultimate responsibility for policy comes back to elected

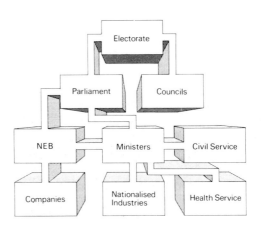

representatives of the public in Parliament or on local councils. True, this accountability in theory can be very different in practice. Many important decisions are taken by management with no involvement of these elected representatives of the public. The point still remains however that there is a potential clash between political and industrial systems of representation if unions seek major influence over policy decisions.

Policy making and policy implementation

We made a distinction earlier between policy making and policy implementation, which are really two separate parts of the management function.

Of course 'owners' as well as management can be involved in policy-making, and this point is particularly important in relation to the public sector, where ministers tend to set policy guide lines. We saw in the last chapter that strong arguments have been put forward in the private sector for the extension of trade union involvement from policy implementation into policy making. So lets try and summarise some of the key arguments and see to what extent they are equally valid for workers in the public sector.

(a) All policy decisions affect workers

Policy decisions that might at first appear to have little to do with workers can, over time, have a very basic impact on the conditions and job security of workers. There is clearly no difference here for public and private sector workers. As the TUC commented in 'Industrial Democracy'.

'At present it is possible for Ministers to advocate policies which could produce redundancy, dispersal, hiving-off, radical technological change, chronic overtime, without the staff who will be affected being able to contribute their point of view early enough to influence the crucial decisions'.

(b) Workers have practical knowledge and expertise to contribute to policy-making

INDUSTRIAL
DEMOCRACY

NATIONAL AND LOCAL GOVERNMENT OFFICERS
ASSOCIATION
1977

Often the best people to decide what policies will or will not work are the workers who will have to implement them. And this goes for workers in both sectors. It might indeed be argued that in the public sector this expertise is even more important, since the elected policy-makers may have little experience of particular industries or services. NALGO has commented that 'given the expertise of many local authority workers, the public could benefit from the contribution that would be made by industrial democracy in local government'. (NALGO 'Industrial Democracy' 1977)

(c) Workers should have equal rights with the providers of capital

We saw in the last chapter that trade unions have argued that private companies should have an obligation to workers as well as to shareholders who provide capital. For while shareholders invest their capital in enterprises, workers invest their livelihoods. Some trade unionists have taken this a stage further and argued that workers and shareholders should have the same rights to representation on the policy making boards of companies. While in the case of the public sector it is the state that provides the capital, the position of the worker is just the same.

(d) Worker involvement in policy-making increases accountability

In law, the managers of a private company are accountable to the shareholders at the annual general meeting of the company. In practice, the shareholders control of the company has often ceased to be meaningful; dissatisfied shareholders sell their shares rather than attempt to change the management. Thus, increasingly, the large corporation is no longer accountable to anybody except itself. The argument for increasing industrial democracy is that a company should at least be accountable to the representatives of the workforce, who are in any case likely to be more representative of the general public than the small group of major shareholders.

But in the public sector, the decision makers are in theory *already* accountable to the wider public, through MPs or local councillors. It is here that special problems arise when we examine industrial democracy in the public sector.

What we do in this chapter is to look at how this political accountability works in the different parts of the public sector illustrated in the diagram on page 126, and how it affects the trade union role.

National Enterprise Board Companies

The NEB was set up under the Industry Act 1975 and forms a kind of 'bridge' between the public and private sectors. One function of the NEB is the provision of finance for investment to private companies, ensuring at the same time that there is some degree of accountability through the NEB to Parliament for the use of public taxpayers money. Through these industrial financing activities, the NEB acquires shares in companies and acts as a state holding company for these shareholdings and for shareholdings in companies previously acquired by the Government in 'rescue' operations such as the bailing out of Rolls Royce and British Leyland. Trade unionists as well as employers are represented on the NEB. The amount of control the NEB exercises over company policy will depend on whether it is a majority or minority shareholder in the company.

Where there is major NEB involvement in a firm, it must submit its corporate plans to the NEB for scrutiny and approval. Among the firms with NEB involvement are British Leyland, Ferranti, Rolls Royce, Alfred Herbert, Cambridge Instrument Company, ICL, Sinclair Electronics. (You can get more information from the Annual Report and Accounts of the NEB).

The trade unions and the Labour Government have seen the establishment of the NEB as a way of increasing the accountability of companies *both* to the public (through parliament and the machinery of political democracy) *and* to their employees (through an extension of industrial democracy).

The NEB has a duty under the law to promote industrial democracy in the undertakings which it controls. The new participation scheme in British Leyland discussed in Chapter 6 was introduced largely as a result of NEB involvement.

Diagram A opposite uses British Leyland as an example to illustrate how these different 'accountabilities' can operate in practice in an NEB firm. While in *theory* increased political accountability in NEB firms offers opportunities for increased worker involvement particularly in corporate planning and long-term policy making, it is less clear how things will work in practice.

It seems from the NEB report that the NEB has left it up to companies to decide what they mean by 'industrial democracy' and most firms seem to interpret 'industrial democracy' as just 'consultation' when it comes to long term plans — in other words informing workers what management have decided!

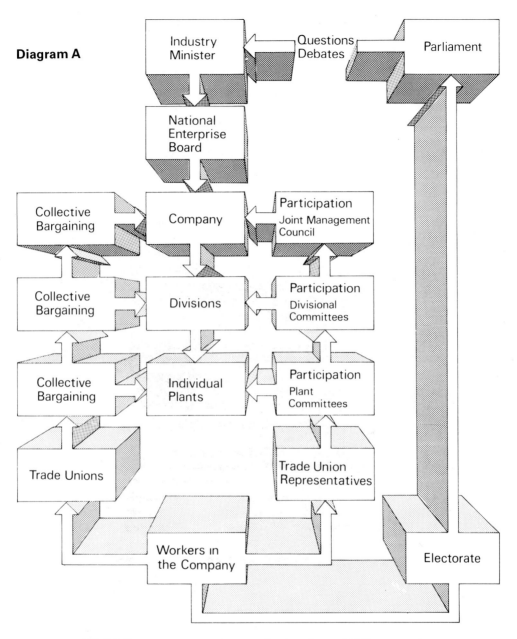

Diagram A

Industry Minister — Questions Debates — Parliament

National Enterprise Board

Collective Bargaining — Company — Participation (Joint Management Council)

Collective Bargaining — Divisions — Participation (Divisional Committees)

Collective Bargaining — Individual Plants — Participation (Plant Committees)

Trade Unions — Trade Union Representatives

Workers in the Company — Electorate

Can you see any reason why the plans of NEB companies should not be the subject of negotiation between unions and management?

Nationalised Industries

In nationalised industries the state owns the corporation assets and appoints a board to operate the industry.

There is normally one trade unionist on the board, but a condition of office is that he or she should have no connections with the industry. The long term policy, particularly in terms of capital investment, is determined by the

Minister through discussions with the Board, while the board is responsible for the day to day running of the industry. The Minister is accountable to Parliament for the overall policies of the nationalised industries. The degree of government control varies with the economic situation prevailing at any one time and the financial viability of the nationalised industry. Normally a nationalised industry needs to seek government approval for price increases and raising external investment funds. The nationalised industries are also subject to examination and detailed questioning by a Parliamentary Select Committee on Nationalised Industries whose reports and recommendations can have considerable influence on government policy. (See Diagram B).

This illustrates that workers in nationalised industries can be even further removed from key policy decisions than workers in private

Diagram B

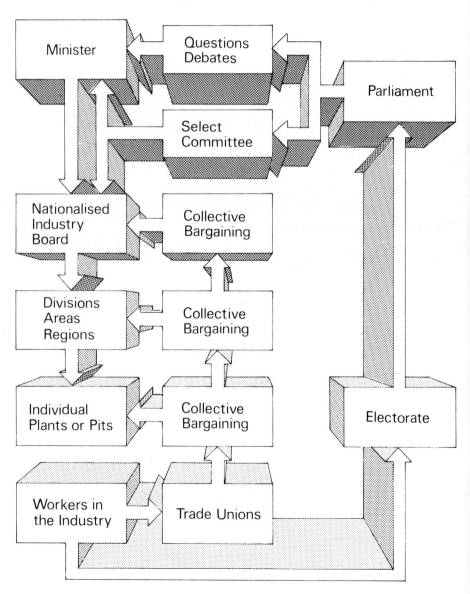

industries. Even if collective bargaining *were* extended to the boardroom, there are important areas of decision making *above* the boardroom. On the other hand it might be argued that because these levels of decision making are part of the more open process of government, they can be more effectively influenced by unions than decisions in private boardrooms.

Can you think of examples where workers in nationalised industries have succeeded in reversing a management decision through pressure on government?

One example was the Government reversal of British Steel plans to close Shotton works.

Shotton workers arrive in London to lobby Parliament.

The Labour Government's approach to the nationalisation of the aircraft and shipbuilding industries in 1976 suggests that nationalisation, like NEB involvement, is seen as a way of increasing accountability *both* to the public *and* to the workforce. The nationalisation acts placed an obligation on the new industries to promote industrial democracy and to put forward concrete plans for this within six months of their establishment.

The question for the trade unions then is, what kind of industrial democracy? Should the trade union approach be any different in the nationalised industries than in the private sector, and if so for what reasons? Lets pick out some of the arguments put forward within the unions. But before you read on, look back at your answer to question 2 at the beginning of the chapter on whether trade unions should be more or less involved in management in the public sector.

What answer did you give and what were your reasons?

AMALGAMATED UNION OF ENGINEERING WORKERS

An Investigation into the Scope of Industrial Democracy

June, 1976

(i) Public ownership as an argument for greater trade union involvement in policy-making.

We saw in the last chapter that some trade unionists take the view that once industry is no longer run for private profit, trade unionists can and should become much more involved and accept a much greater responsibility for policy-making.

For example, the AUEW, while opposed to worker representation on boards in the private sector, calls for *majority* worker representation on boards in the public sector. This is what they have to say in their booklet 'An Investigation into the Scope of Industrial Democracy':

'It is clear that there is a distinction between the private sector being run purely for profit and the public sector which should be run in the interests of the public, and our approach should reflect that difference. There is a major role for trade unions to play in the management of nationalised industries and, in our view, this would be best achieved in each industry by:—

1 Responsibility through a Minister to Parliament.

2 Central control by a single management board, to which trade unionists should be elected in a majority position from both the specific industry concerned and the wider Trade Union Movement.

3 Joint union-management committees at other levels.

4 The right of unions to full information and consultation on plans and policies before decisions are taken.

5 Full recognition of unions to pursue their collective bargaining functions.'

The NUM has put forward proposals extending this principle of majority worker control to the level of each colliery. It proposed that overall management of a colliery should be in the hands of a management team *elected by workers*. Both managers and trade unionists would be eligible for membership of this team.

 Would you as a tax payer and user of nationalised industries approve of majority trade union control of these industries?

What are your views on the AUEW proposal that the trade unionists on the board should be drawn from the wider trade union movement as well as from within the industry in question?

How do you think these proposals would affect collective bargaining practices?

(ii) Public ownership as an argument for restricting trade union involvement in policy-making.

Some trade unionists have argued that nationalised industries exist to serve the community, and therefore the community through its elected representatives in Parliament must have majority, if not total, control of policy-making in these industries.

'In the case of the nationalised industries, we are not setting up workers co-operatives . . .; we are running organisations which are owned by the community, and it is important that the management is responsible to the community and does not have to try to serve two masters'.

J. Glynn, Society of Post Office Executives at Trade Union Congress 1974

From your experience can you think of examples in the nationalised industries of the interests of workers conflicting with the interests of the community?

Can you think of examples where the interests of the community and the interests of the workers are the same?

Would you agree that nationalised industries do serve the community at present?

(iii) Same role for trade unions in private and nationalised industries?

At the 1976 Trades Union Congress the TUC General Secretary spoke out strongly against the 'curious doctrine that the role and position of unions in publicly owned industries is basically different, is fundamentally different, from their role and position in private industry'. In their booklet 'Industrial Democracy', the TUC argued that unions in both private and nationalised industries should be involved in policy-making and should have available to them, as one means of achieving this, a right to 50% representation on the boards of their companies.

If workers were represented on the board of nationalised industries, who should worker representatives be responsible or accountable to?
—the Minister
—the Trade Union members

If worker representatives were responsible to the Minister do you think this would cause conflicts with trade union responsibilities?

If worker representatives were accountable to the membership and not to the Minister, do you think this would be an infringement of political democracy?

Recent experiments

Recent proposals for extensions in industrial democracy in two publicly owned industries suggest that the Government takes the view that the accountability of *all* board members to the public through the Minister and Parliament must be maintained.

In Harland and Wolff agreement has been reached on a new 15 man board comprising—

one third trade union representatives, one third management representatives, and one third independent Government appointees.

In the Post Office, agreement has been reached on a new 20 man board comprising—

seven trade union representatives, seven management representatives, five independents, and a non-executive chairman.

All board members, workers included, would be technically appointed by the Minister and accountable to the Minister, although in practice the unions would elect their representatives and put forward those elected as nominees whom the Minister would then appoint.

What would your reaction be to such a scheme?

Do you think the presence of 'independent' members is a good way of safeguarding community interests?

Ministers' powers

Even if workers were represented on the board of nationalised industries, we have already seen that they would still not be in a position to influence those aspects of policy that are determined at ministerial level. This is one reason why the TUC has argued for the setting up of committees that bring together representatives of unions and management with the relevant minister to discuss broad policy for certain nationalised industries. A commission covering the energy sector has recently been set up, comprising 7 representatives of energy industry management, 7 representatives of the TUC Fuel and Power Industries Committee, representatives of industry and representatives of other consumers, with the Secretary of State for Energy in the chair. It gives unions a chance to discuss with the Minister the long-term plans of the various energy industries, and to see that these plans co-ordinate into some wider national plan for energy.

Do you think there should or can be the same approach to extending industrial democracy in all nationalised industries?

(If you look at the NALGO booklet 'Industrial Democracy' you will see that NALGO members in different nationalised industries have come up with different approaches to Industrial Democracy.)

Health Service

Chapter 6 referred briefly to the control and decision making structure of the health service with its tiers of district health authorities, area health authorities, regional health authorities, and final responsibility with the Minister for Health and Social Security. (See diagram C opposite). The 'interface' with political democracy takes place as in the nationalised industries through accountability to the Minister and Parliament. However, the role of the Minister in terms of overall policy-making is *more extensive* in the health service than in the nationalised industries. The budget powers and responsibilities of the regional health authorities are quite closely defined by the Minister. The RHA's plan and allocate regional services within these defined budgets — and the kinds of decisions they make about expanding or running down particular services, or building new facilities could be of great importance for trade unionists, as well as for the community in terms of meeting community health needs. You will see from the diagram that there is no collective bargaining machinery at present at regional level. A recent report by Lord McCarthy on the Health Service called 'Making Whitley Work' has recommended the establishment of Regional Whitley Councils to help fill this gap.

Regional and Area Health Authorities

Who sits on these bodies and how do they get there?

At present all members of regional health authorities are appointed by the Minister, after 'consultation with interested organisations' which would include trade unions, as well as local authorities, health professions and universities.

In their evidence to the Royal Commission on the Health Service, the TUC argued that this present situation was in fact highly unsatisfactory from the viewpoint of both political *and* industrial democracy. They suggested that accountability both to the public and to employees would be more effective

MAKING WHITLEY WORK

A review of the operation of the National Health Service Whitley Council System

by
Lord McCarthy

Fellow of Nuffield College and Oxford Management Centre

Department of Health and Social Security

Diagram C

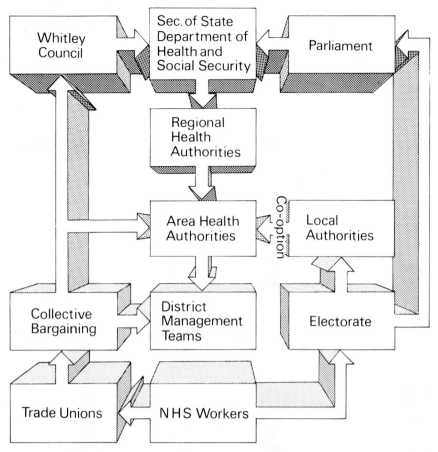

if members of these bodies were more directly accountable to local interests, rather than merely appointed by the Minister. Accordingly they proposed that

'half of the members of a regional authority should be appointed by the district or metropolitan district authorities within the region, and half elected by independent recognised trade unions being representative both of workers within the service as well as the interests of workers more generally as members of the public'.

In the case of area health authorities, there is provision at present for four members to be appointed by the relevant local authority, but the rest (the majority) are appointed by the regional health authority, again in consultation with interested organisations. The TUC argued that these bodies should also be reconstituted on the same lines advocated for regional health authorities, giving 50% trade union representation.

The argument the TUC is making is one we have come across already in this chapter — that the changes would improve accountability both to the local public using the service, and to the workers employed by the service. The TUC does not see any conflict between these two objectives.

The TUC argue above that worker representation should include trade unionists from *outside* the health service, representing the interests of workers as members of the public. The TUC does *not* recommend

135

this for nationalised industries.

Can you see any valid reasons for this difference of approach?

A strong argument from the workers' side for increasing trade union representation on these decision-making bodies is that doctors and nurses have long been represented in their 'professional' capacity. But what this means in trade union terms is that some privileged groups of workers are given the opportunity to influence decisions that affect the future of all workers in the service.

 Can you think of any valid reasons why doctors and nurses should be represented and not other workers?

Recent developments

As with the nationalised industries, the Government appear reluctant to move to 50% trade union involvement on decision-making bodies. In 1975, however, the Secretary of State proposed that two representatives of those working in the NHS, other than doctors and nurses, should be elected to RHAs and AHAs.

One very practical problem raised here is, given the very large number of staff organisations recognised in the Health Service, how to devise a fair system of electing only two representatives.

NUPE members protest about government policy on health service expenditure

Influencing Ministerial policy

If trade unions in the Health Service really want to influence policy-making, then, just as in the nationalised industries, there is a need for some kind of discussion forum with the relevant Minister. In the report 'Making Whitley Work', Lord McCarthy suggested this was a major gap in existing bargaining and consultation machinery. He advocates the establishment of a national forum where 'consultation on strategic planning can take place between the Department of Health and recognised staff organisations'.

This would extend consultation, if not bargaining, to cover major policy issues.

Do you see ways in which collective bargaining could be extended to cover all aspects of policy in the health service?

Local authorities

In the local authorities the tensions between political and industrial democracy are greater. For those who make policy within the local authorities — the councillors — are not just accountable to the Minister, like other examples we have looked at; they are themselves actually elected representatives of the local public.

So what kind of influence can workers demand on policy without distorting the political balance of local democracy? Can local authority employees justifiably make demands for representation on policy bodies within the authority? This is what Alan Fisher of NUPE had to say at the 1976 Trades Union Congress:

'We must reconcile the conflict that exists between civic democracy and industrial democracy. While a case could be made for having half the local council elected by those who work for it, I think this could clearly frustrate the political choice of the electorate which is an essential part of our present system'.

It would certainly seem that if workers as employees had voting rights on councils they would in effect become privileged members of the public with *two* votes in local politics. But is the issue as straightforward as this in reality?

To answer this we need to look more closely at how local authorities operate.

Diagram D

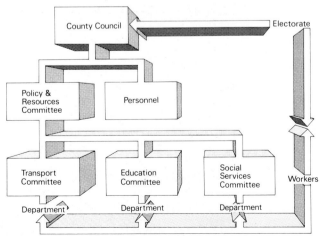

137

In theory at any rate it is the council with its elected councillors that makes policy. Committees have the function of implementing policy, and putting forward policy proposals for ratification by the council. But, as we have already seen in chapter 6, committees, especially the policy and resources committee, can have a very strong effect on council policy.

And not all members of council committees are elected representatives of the public. Chief officers or managers appointed by the councillors also take part in committees, doing most of the work in exploring policy options which part-time councillors, who are also lay people, may not be able to do.

So while *in theory* actual policy decisions are supposed to rest purely with elected councillors, *in practice* it is difficult to maintain such clear distinctions. Indeed the Bains report, which we saw in chapter 6 advocated a new corporate approach to planning in local government, actually recommended a relaxation of this separation between the jobs of appointed officers and elected members.

'We believe that if local government is to have any chance of achieving a corporate approach to its affairs, members and officers must both recognise that neither can regard any area of the authorities' work and administration as exclusively theirs . . . Members must realise that the skilled professional officer is not just a servant who is paid to do as he is told'.

 How do you think this affects the argument for workers being more involved in council policy-making?

Certainly it can be argued that at present, policy is *not* just the pure preserve of elected members. Professional managers (who are also incidentally trade unionists) have a very strong influence on this policy. So why not other trade unionists who can have expertise to contribute just as managers have?

But it is usually suggested that worker representation on councils would operate against the public interest.

 How would you respond to this argument?

Here are some points for argument often made in discussions about this:

After members of the public have put a cross on their ballot paper, they tend to have little further influence on their elected representatives. Could workers be in a much better position to exert continuous influence and monitor how councillors are fulfilling their election pledges?

Even where the public are involved through public inquiries etc., they may have little inside or technical knowledge to help them assess the arguments of the 'experts'. Again, might council workers be better placed here to 'counterbalance' the experts and help stimulate public debate?

Union policy

What conclusions have unions come to about worker representation in local authorities?

No public service union has decided to press the idea that workers should have 50% voting rights on councils. NALGO however have argued that workers should have a non-voting presence on councils:

'Whilst recognising the democratic basis of local councils NALGO believes that basically workers have a right to be involved in the policy-decision making of employers in both the public and private sector . . . at the level of the full council NALGO considers that worker representatives should have the right to speak and influence decision-making but should not have voting rights and by this means would not disturb the balance of political power of the local authority'

NALGO: Industrial Democracy 1977

The Town Hall: The next stage for an extension of industrial democracy?

The TUC Local Government Committee which includes all unions involved in this area has come to a slightly different conclusion. The committee decided against *any* form of worker involvement in the full council. Policy-making would be left to elected representatives. What the TUC have pressed for is worker representation at the level of council committees. On committees, like policy and resources committees, transport committees, direct work committees, and lower level bodies like school and college management committees, the TUC policy adopted in 1974 was that workers should have a *maximum of 20% representation with voting rights*, with a minimum of two representatives. Where committees covered one department only, representatives would be drawn from and elected by trade unionists in that department. Where committees covered more than one department, like the policy and resources committee, representatives would be elected by all trade unionists in the local authority. The Local

Government Committee argued to the Government that any distortion of 'political balance' caused by workers having voting rights on these committees could if necessary be 'adjusted' when the decisions went to full council for ratification.

Catching up with the teachers?

In fact teachers have had representation with voting rights on education committees for the past 70 years. Rather like the doctors in the National Health Service, they were admitted to committees chiefly in a professional capacity in the first place. But teachers are also trade unionists as well as professionals.

What is needed now, the TUC has argued, is an extension of this principle so that *all* workers in education establishments can influence policy, and so that teachers are not in the sometimes difficult position of making decisions in isolation on policies that can have a very real effect on the conditions of other groups of workers.

 Do you think that minority representation with voting power on council committees would be a help to trade unionists?

(Look back at some of the arguments in the last chapter for and against worker representation on company boards — do you think these arguments are still valid for the public sector?)

A joint initiative by the TUC/Labour Party

In discussions with the TUC in 1974/5 the Labour Party took the view that for workers to have voting rights even on council committees would be an infringement of political democracy. They argued that these committees *do* make policy decisions, and although in theory all such decisions go to the Council for ratification, this is often a mere formality. There is no time for full discussion in Council.

In 1976 the TUC Local Government Committee and the Labour Party set up a joint working party to try and resolve their differences. The Joint Statement emerging from this working party is reproduced in the NALGO booklet Industrial Democracy. It was endorsed by the TUC Local Government Committee and so now represents TUC policy. It calls for 20% worker representation *with no voting rights* on council committees. It suggests that the major development of industrial democracy in local authorities must be at lower levels, and recommends the more systematic establishment of departmental committees.

 What do you think of the TUC/Labour party proposals?
Do you think they would be more or less effective from a trade union view point than the original TUC demand for voting rights on committees?

Experiments

If workers do not seek voting rights on either councils or council committees, there is no need to wait for legislation before experiments in new forms of worker involvement can be tried.

The Greater London Council set up a Members Working Party on Industrial Democracy in 1975 and it reported in 1976. The Working Party's proposals, which were not supported by the minority of Conservative members can be summarised as follows:

Representations should be made to the Government for amending legislation to permit employees to become non-voting members of committees and sub-committees. Pending such legislation employee representatives should have a standing invitation to attend and speak at the main GLC and ILEA committees, other than the Establishment and Finance Boards. Employee representatives should number not more than one-third of the membership of each committee as currently constituted.

Basildon council too initiated an experiment in 1975 whereby union representatives could attend and speak at council main committees, and at full council meetings. This experiment and its results were illustrated and discussed in detail in the TU Studies film 'Servants of the Public?'

 Has the possibility of such experiments ever been discussed in your local council?

The Role of Government
While a local council is responsible for financial policy and administration, the *amount of finance* is largely determined by national government decisions. So once again, as with other public sector organisations, important aspects of policy are determined at Government level.

 What kind of influence if any do you think local authority workers should have over Government policy that affects the financial situation of local authorities?

(Look back at some of the proposals put forward for influencing Minister's decisions in other public services)

Civic rights for local authority workers
Both the 1933 and 1972 Local Government Acts prevent local authority employees from standing for office in their employing authorities.

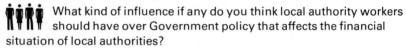 Can you see any valid reason for this disqualification?

The TUC in their 1974 policy statement urged that these legislative restrictions should be removed so that all local authority employees (with the exception of chief officers and their deputies) can stand for office in local council elections. The 1976 joint TUC/Labour Party statement takes a similar approach.

The Civil Service
The tensions we saw between political and industrial democracy in local government come up again, magnified if anything, when we look at the civil service. If civil service unions were to demand representation on the policy-making bodies affecting their members, they would be demanding representation on parliamentary committees, in the cabinet and in Parliament itself.

 How would you respond as a citizen to such a demand?

Most people would probably regard such a demand as an infringement of political democracy, and indeed this is the view that has been taken by the civil service unions. The Staff Side of the Civil Service National Whitley Council commented in a note submitted to the Government that —

'In the special circumstances of the Civil Service we are not seeking membership of the bodies concerned with the formulation of Government policy . . . (Our) proposals respect the accountability of Ministers to Parliament and of Parliament to the electorate'.

But this does not mean that the civil service unions have given up hope on influencing policy-making. In the civil service, just as in local government, senior staff already have a very strong influence on policy. Once more practice does not always coincide with theory, and while Ministers are supposed to control civil servants many people would argue that the *top* civil servants control Ministers.

What the civil service unions want is to increase the influence of *all* their members over the formulation of policies that affect their interests. They have stressed the need for more effective disclosure of information and 'the fullest possible prior consultation regarding the make-up of estimates, including cash limits, imminent new legislation, and the proposed location or relocation of work, in so far as they affect the interests of the staff'.

On disclosure of information the unions recognise that a major reason for seeking representation on policy making bodies in the private and the public sector is to get better access to information. They conclude that 'in the Civil Service, this gap will need to be filled by the Official Side taking alternative steps to ensure that full information is made available. This will remove any fear that, by acting in secrecy, the Civil Service management is seeking to avoid its responsibilities in the field of industrial democracy'.

Whitley Bulletin, Feb. 1977

Sponsoring MPs
We have seen that the common problem faced by all public sector employees is that some fundamental aspects of policy are determined *outside* the employing organisation, by Government ministers. We have already looked at a number of proposals for extending union influence over Ministers' decisions. Where a union sponsors MPs, this can provide another channel of influence.

Some unions with sponsored MPs have regular meetings between these MPs and the union's executive to discuss issues that the union wants to raise in Parliament, or to discuss union policy towards issues that are currently being debated.

Most union rule books make it clear that sponsored MPs cannot be mandated to vote in a particular way. A union can make sure that their MPs are aware of union policies, but after that it is very much up to the individual MPs.

 Do you think that sponsored MPs should be made to vote according to union policy — e.g. by withdrawing sponsorship if they fail to do this?

Action checklist

● Find out if any developments in industrial democracy are taking place within your local council. Raise the issue for discussion if possible within your Trades Council.

● If you work in the public sector, discuss the issues raised in this chapter within your branch or shop stewards committee. You could arrange for a showing of the TU Studies film 'Servants of the Public?' illustrating what was done at Basildon Council, as a stimulus to interest and discussion. (To obtain film, see page 183).

● If you see advantages in being represented in the relevant policy making body in your industry or service, draw up a list of powers and safeguards which would have to built into a system of representation before you as a trade unionist were prepared to become involved in it.

● Discuss

a how seats on the policy-making body would be allocated between various unions or groups of workers (where there are a large number of unions it may not be possible for every union to be represented individually)

b what new forms of union organisation might be needed to back up this representation on the policy-making body (e.g. the workers council proposed by NALGO and referred to in chapter 6)

c the machinery through which worker representatives would report back to the people they represent.

● If you are opposed to trade union representation on policy-making bodies, discuss what strategies you need to adopt in order to improve your access to management information and extend union influence over planning decisions, e.g.

the negotiation of information agreements with management.

the establishment of new collective bargaining, or consultation machinery.

● Discuss how trade union influence on Ministerial level decisions could be improved within your industry or service.

Further reading

TUC 'Industrial Democracy'

NALGO 'Industrial Democracy' 1977

'Making Whitley Work — A Review of the operation of the National Health Service Whitley Council System' Lord McCarthy, Department of Health & Social Security 1976.

Whitley Bulletin (Journal of the Civil Service National Whitley Council) Feb. 1977.

NEB Annual Report and Accounts, 1976.

Chapter 9   Making Union Democracy Work

'The essential characteristic of all trade unions is that they are responsible to the work people themselves who comprise their membership.'
TUC 'Trade Unionism'.

Introduction

Trade Unions seek to extend democracy at work by increasing their influence over management decisions. So it's very important that unions themselves are democratic. Unions are often criticised — particularly by outsiders and on the media — on the grounds that they are not democratic enough. One aim of this chapter is to set these criticisms in perspective, and to help you work out your own replies to them. It is more important though, to direct efforts into developing and improving the democracy within the trade union movement. Unions frequently revise and amend their rulebooks, and review their structure and organisation, with this aim in mind. A major aim of this chapter is to help you play a greater part in these debates. The chapter therefore deals with issues like:

- Democracy in the workplace union organisation.
- Trade union policy making at national level.
- Union constitutions and rule books.
- Trade Union branches.
- Full-time officials, elected or appointed?
- Postal ballots.
- The closed shop.
- 'Factions' in unions.
- Relationships between unions.

While reading the chapter you will find it helpful if you have a copy of your union rulebook with you.

Questions

Note down your answers to these questions before watching the television programme or working through the chapter.

Yes   No

☐   ☐   **1** Do you have union meetings for members at your own place of work?

2 How much information do you receive about union activities and policies
a Locally
b Nationally.

☐   ☐   **3** Do you attend union branch meetings?
☐   ☐   Do you feel that branch business is relevant to your own trade union interests?

4 Are full-time officials in your union

☐ Elected

☐ Appointed

Yes No

☐ ☐ **5** Is it democractic that members should have the right to disregard a majority vote for strike action?

☐ ☐ **6** Should union members have the right to campaign against existing union policies?

7 What is your view of union closed shops? . . . .
. . . .
. . . .
. . . .

8 Do you know how your union decided its policy on the Social Contract?

What is Union 'Democracy'?

Practically everyone assumes that unions *ought* to be democratic. But there are disagreements about what 'being democratic' actually means. Because of this it is very easy to attack the trade union movement for falling short on 'democracy'. After all, it's often the people who complain about lack of democracy when they don't like what union leaders are doing who are the first to complain about lack of leadership when they don't like what the members are doing.

At the outset of this chapter, then, you may need to think what is meant in speaking of union democracy. There are at least three main issues to consider.

Collective Strength or Individual Rights?

One of the main functions of a union is to act as a 'pressure group' to further the common interests of the members. This requires a measure of organisation, discipline and acceptance of majority decisions. On the other hand, democracy within the unions involves the members' right to a say over policy decisions, and the right to disagree with, and argue against decisions. It involves the right to be treated fairly by the union where discipline is concerned, the right to be informed about union business and so on. We must keep these two aspects of democracy in balance. For example, if we stress in isolation the individual rights of members, we may find that collective strength has been undermined. On the other hand, just looking at the 'collective' aspects of union democracy might lead to too much centralisation and not enough opportunity for individual members to have their say.

Active or Passive democracy?

Some people see democracy as voting for representatives and then giving them the right to take all the decisions in their name. (This is often the way the democratic role of Members of Parliament is described and justified). This could be called 'passive democracy'.

On the other hand, it might be said that this is not enough. Other ideas about democracy have stressed the importance of members' participation, activity and involvement on a more continuous basis. Certainly most trade unionists feel that the democratic health of their organisation rests mainly on the quality and quantity of *participation* by members in the work of the union. This can promote collective organisation at the same time as helping to increase the amount of say which individual rank and file members have.

Efficiency or Democracy?

You may feel that democracy in unions is 'all very well' but that, when it comes down to it, there is a job to be done. Decisions have to be made, delays have to be avoided, union representatives have to accept responsibilities and give the membership a lead. At one level this may be partly true. Have you ever heard a fellow trade unionist say that

'The best committee consists of two people with one person absent'?

If you are a shop steward, do you ever feel under pressure to make agreements with management without full reference back to your members?

Conducting elections may be administratively time-consuming, as may be arrangements for improving the circulation of information, or the process of referring back agreements for ratification before they are implemented. But taking short cuts doesn't always help efficiency in the long run. The most sensible policy, as seen by trade union leaders, will be of limited value if it fails to win the support of the union's membership. In any event, the job of the trade union movement it not just to make decisions, but to implement them. This cannot be done without the use of the union's major resource — the active involvement and support of the membership at large. We cannot use narrow 'business oriented' concepts of efficiency when discussing the effectiveness of unions. Democracy is a vital part of the operation of trade unions. It is not a luxury which can be sacrificed in order to make the unions more 'efficient'.

Jack Jones, the General Secretary of the Transport and General Workers Union put it like this:

'Many people have talked as if all we had to do in the trade union movement was to streamline ourselves — modernise the structure — and become more commercial and 'businesslike'. More experts, more professionals, more computers . . . but that is only the fringe'.

Unions depend on democracy and involvement to produce the army of lay officials and activists which keep the movement going. Union leaders rely on the democratic expression of members' wishes in order to discover which policies will meet with support, and which will not. The active support of union members is essential if the policies and aims of the trade union movement are to be achieved.

Union democracy at the workplace

At workplace level the problem of ensuring that unions function democratically is relatively easier to tackle. Most shop stewards are elected annually, although many are not opposed by other contenders. Report-back meetings of members can be quickly arranged, and it is easier to keep in touch with new developments. Members are represented by fellow workers who share their problems and know their views.

There may be difficulties, however, even at this level. Consider your own workplace organisation. Do you face any of these problems?

Lack of volunteers and low involvement may make it hard to develop an effective system of representation.

Workplaces may be too small or fragmented for good communication to develop.

In very large plants there may be some lack of contact between senior stewards and members, or certain groups may feel that their interests are neglected or 'crowded out' by the problems of other groups.

Some groups, for instance women workers, immigrants, part-time workers or shift workers, may find it hard to get involved.

For the most part, however, problems at this level *can* be tackled in order to improve union democracy. Participation is easier to arrange, and communications can be improved. The workers will have a common identity and will feel that union business at this level is *relevant* to them.

Most members will only be involved in the union at workplace level, and it is very important that democracy and participation should function effectively there.

A number of unions in recent years have argued that, as well as developing workplace organisation and involvement, unions should positively attempt to decentralise so as to increase the extent of real involvement available to trade unionists at local level.

Look again at the quote from Jack Jones printed above. He went on to say that —

'Our success — and indeed the success of industry itself is going to be determined by the extent to which we can decentralise — spread decision-making amongst the workpeople, and above all get industrial agreements settled where they are going to be operated, that is the key.'

Trade Unionism in the Seventies, TGWU

Can you think of any ways in which your union organisation at workplace level could be improved to strengthen participation and involvement? (The checklist at the end of the chapter may give you some ideas.)

Are there any decisions taken above workplace level in your union at the moment which you feel you could decide more effectively at a lower level?

Trade Unions above workplace level

When trade unions first started in the last century there were few problems in ensuring that everyone was fully involved. All the decisions could be taken locally, all members could have equal chance of a say. But we can't improve union democracy by just wishing for the 'good old days'. Unions need to have national organisation extending far beyond the workplace.

Before reading on note down what reasons you would give for this.

Here are some suggested reasons.

1 To promote unity between workers in different areas, companies and

National Headquarters of the Railwaymens' Union

industries to develop better, coordinated policies with more strength behind them.

2 To develop the finances and resources needed to operate efficiently without duplication of effort.

3 To conduct negotiations at company and industry level covering many workplaces.

4 To deal with the government, both on its policies and on legislation affecting working people.

Have Trade Unions become 'bureaucratic'?

The extension and development of trade union organisation has posed three major challenges for effective trade union democracy.

a The development of large scale trade union organisation has resulted in big increases in the number of full time officers dealing with negotiations, administration and research. These are professional trade unionists with far more time and resources to devote to union work than most lay members. It is sometimes said that this gives them a disproportionate influence over union affairs, and that they can become separated by their position from the feelings and aspirations of the membership of their unions. On the other hand, almost all full-time officials have had long experience as lay members of their unions, and are never in a position to go against the majority wishes of their members for prolonged periods of time.

b Particular groups of members may feel that their wishes receive less recognition in an organisation containing many groups of workers. For example, members of a small union involved in a 'merger' of unions may feel that they have lost some of their influence over union policy.

c Union members may tend to be less interested in the wider business of their unions, and concentrate only on those aspects of union work which are immediately relevant, such as local collective bargaining and workplace union organisation. As a result, participation in union work above the workplace may fall off — branch meetings may become less well attended and communications between members and their union structure may become more difficult.

Do you feel that any of these problems affect your own union?

Can you think of any ways of tackling them?

Is it important that members should have some knowledge of the trade union movement outside their workplace?

The Union Constitution

The *way* in which unions take the views of their membership and transform these into policies and action is, of course, influenced by their constitutions or rule-books. Constitutions take many shapes or forms, but most involve union *branches* of members, a national conference of delegates from branches, and an *executive committee* elected from the branches. In addition many unions have 'Trade Groups' at national levels which deal with the affairs of members in particular industries, subject to National Conference and Executive Council policies. Also many unions have committees set up at regional level which are based on delegations from branches and district committees.

An outline union structure might look something like this:

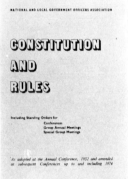

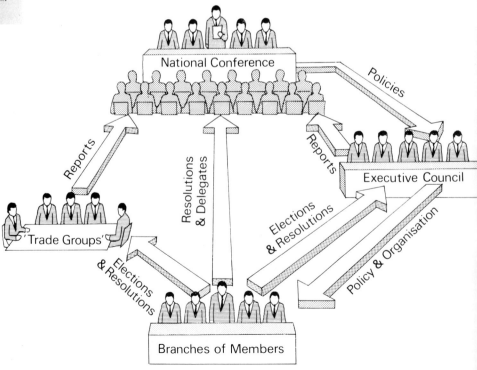

This structure would operate by

1 Branches sending resolutions and delegates to conference. Conference makes the policies which determine how the Executive proceeds.

2 In between conferences the executive is responsible for implementing conference policies. If new situations emerge, the Executive may take a new initiative. Then it would be responsible to the subsequent conference to justify the steps it had taken.

3 Branches have further opportunities to influence the executive by sending resolutions, and perhaps by electing their own executive members for their regions. Executives may from time to time refer decisions back to branches or members in between conferences.

Look at your own rulebook. Is it broadly similar to the outline description above? What differences can you see?

Do you have any form of 'Trade Groups' or committees dealing with just one industry in your union?

Is your executive committee elected by the branches of the union?

How are delegates to National Conference chosen?

Critics of the trade union movement have often said that unions fail to live up to the model outlined above. For instance, branches may be poorly attended, elections may suffer from lack of information about candidates, conferences may be influenced by union executives through the platform and the process of 'compositing' or grouping resolutions. Information about policy options may not reach the membership at large in sufficient quantities to enable them to make informed choices.

But the truth of such general criticisms is not always simple. This may become clearer in considering the following points:

The leadership of trade unions is rarely made up of a united 'bureaucracy' opposed to the 'rank and file' membership; there will be divisions among the leadership which reflect divisions of opinion among the members of the union.

Even though participation rates at union *branch meetings* are typically not high, a large proportion of union activity happens at *workplace level,* where members are usually better represented and able to put their viewpoint to their officials. In some cases they may act independently of their union's leadership.

Union leaders have both formal and informal ways of judging the feelings of their members. While they may try and put over their own point of view, they will rarely stand out in opposition to clear membership feelings. In any event, it is by no means uncommon for union executives to be defeated at conferences.

Many of the criticisms made against unions reflect the problems experienced in practice by all democratic organisations. Of course unions, like all organisations, have their share of fallible people and those working for their own ends. It's also true that the need for action or decision in the face of events often allows too little time for wide-ranging debate and voting by all branches. But these same practical considerations affect all our political parties, which are usually held to be among the most democratically organised in the world.

Much can be done to improve communications, participation and involvement in the unions. It is still true however, that the democratic credentials of the British trade union movement can stand comparisons with any other institutions in our society. Meetings of shareholders for example, occur only annually, and have far lower rates of participation than do trade union branch meetings. The Bullock Report on industrial democracy had this to say about shareholders' meetings:—

'In practice of course, particularly in large public companies, the shareholders are often a passive force, exercising their powers on the advice and initiative of the board of directors and rarely initiating action themselves. This is not to say that the shareholders' powers are not important in a few unusual cases, nor to imply that the shareholders are in some way manipulated or bypassed by their directors. It is inevitable that where the shareholders are numerous and diverse, they will in many cases be insufficiently organised and interested to do more than leave the detailed business of the company to a board of directors and to professional managers.'

Current debates about trade union democracy
The following section reviews some current issues and arguments about trade union democracy.

The Trade Union Branch
'Branch life may become disconnected from membership interests, especially if it is a "composite" branch made up of many different elements. One of the most serious problems of this kind may stem from the lack of connection between branch and place of work.'
John Hughes 'Trade Union Structure and Government'

Branches are theoretically the key link in the chain between the members and the union's policy-making structure. Yet often branches are not well attended — perhaps less than 10% of the membership. If this is so then elections and delegations from the branch may be remote from the majority of the membership. The fact that unions do rather well in terms of attendance in contrast to most other voluntary institutions is no cause for complacency.

Many strategies have been put forward to improve this situation.

1 'Workplace branches' have been suggested as a way of tackling the separation between workplace and branch, thus making the branch more relevant as a focus of local union activity. Members would identify more with the work of branch and would thus be drawn more fully into the operation of unions' consitutional machinery. The branch could meet at or near work and would be more accessible, for example, to women or shift-workers. This strategy has proved successful in larger workplaces but in situations where there are a large number of unions, and Joint Shop Stewards Committees deal with many of the negotiating issues, a workplace branch may still find it hard to complete for attention.

2 Some unions have attempted to increase attendance by making branch business more interesting — for example, by inviting visiting speakers or widening the discussion to include the policy options and issues checklisted in TU Studies Books. (See suggestions on pp 6-7, 175, 182-3). USDAW has attempted to develop the role of its branches by convening regular regional meetings of branch delegates and encouraging the 'federation' of local branches for educational and social purposes.

3 Another approach is rather different. Instead of concentrating attention on the branch as the only constitutional link between members and the union, some unions have tried to give constitutional powers (e.g. to send delegates or submit resolutions) to committees of shop stewards. The AUEW and NUPE have done this to a certain extent. The argument in favour of this approach is that elected stewards committees provide a more effective and representative body for receiving reports and instructing delegates than do many branch meetings. This might also be a way of breaking down the division between local collective bargaining and the wider trade union. It is also argued that far more members would have some contact with the work of the union outside the workplace if this was the subject of reports from stewards than they would through a branch meeting. Nevertheless, the branch must be kept in existence to provide opportunity for mass membership involvement when this is needed.

How many members attend your branch meetings?
Can you think of any ways of improving the relevance of your own branch structure for the membership?

Should members who do not attend branch meetings be refused information about branch activities?

The Selection of Full-time Officials

In some unions, notably the AUEW, the full-time officials are elected regularly. In the NUM and NUR they are elected on first taking up office. In the GMWU appointed officials are endorsed by a vote of the members they cover after a probationary period. In other unions, for example, NUPE, NALGO, ASTMS and TGWU appointments are made by the Executive or sub-committee of the executive. The EETPU has recently moved from a system of election to appointment by the Executive. In some unions, for example, the TGWU and GMWU, only the general secretaries are elected by the votes of the membership.

Some trade unionists feel that the regular election of all full-time officials would improve union democracy, and there are many arguments for and against this practice.

The basic argument *for* election is that officials should be accountable to the membership they serve. There is a danger, it is said, that officials by the nature of their jobs may become less close to the feelings of their members. Officials are in powerful positions and should be accountable for the use of this power. It is also argued that direct responsibility of officials to the executive of their union gives the executive additional resources and control in any situation where groups of members and the executive might come into conflict.

The arguments *against* election are more varied.

'The appointment of officials does not necessarily imply lack of democracy if officials are under the control of lay committees which in turn are freely elected by the membership.'

R. Fletcher, 'Problems of Trade Union Democracy' — Institute for Workers Control

According to this argument it may be no less democratic, in practice, if officials are reporting to committees of lay members which monitor their activities and instruct them on a regular basis, rather than if they are simply accountable through the more intermittent and haphazard process of election.

In many unions it is regarded as unfair to demand that officials shall work under the insecurity of an elected job. Unlike many members of parliament, if they were defeated they might have difficulty returning to their old jobs either because of the reputation they had built up as trade unionists, or because they had given up promotion possibilities to work for the union. Furthermore, it is argued that if officials are denied any voice in the making of policy, as formally they are in many unions, then it is unfair for them to be judged by the policies which they have to implement.

In addition, it is sometimes said that elected officials could be tempted to neglect small branches and pockets of membership and concentrate on those areas which can produce larger votes.

There are thus powerful arguments for and against the election of full-time officials. However, even those who oppose elections often argue that there must be procedures whereby members' complaints about officials can be taken up and given a hearing.

 Do you think that it would be right for your own union to elect all its full-time officials?

What is your view of appointing officials for life?

Examine your union rulebook. To whom are your Full-time Officers responsible?

Postal Ballots

A number of unions, notably the AUEW and the EETPU, have in recent years adopted the 'Postal Ballot' as a way of conducting union elections. This means that each member receives a voting paper by post and completes and returns it privately. The alternative to this system is normally to conduct elections by votes taken publicly by show of hands at branch meetings.

The main argument in favour of postal ballots is that it increases the rate of participation in union elections. This is generally true, given the relatively low attendance rates at branch meetings. For instance, in 1968, under the branch voting system, only 11% of the AUEW's membership voted in the election for General Secretary. In 1975 38% of the membership voted in postal ballots for national officials. Postal ballots may also reduce the chances of abuse of electoral procedures, and since voting is secret, are likely to reduce the amount of 'pressure' on the voter from fellow union members.

Despite this apparent advantage in terms of involvement, it is still argued that postal balloting is less democratic than it appears. For one thing, while increasing the *quantity* of participation, it does not do much about the 'quality' of involvement.

You may remember that the introduction to this chapter discussed the difference between 'active' and 'passive' theories of democracy. Which of these theories best describes the system of postal balloting?

In a union meeting, decisions are taken in the light of discussion and debate at the meeting. In a postal ballot many members may not have full information about candidates, and, so opponents of postal ballots argue, the press and the media have been able to use this as an opportunity to interfere in the elections by selectively publicising certain candidates.

There are also administrative arguments about postal balloting — that it may be expensive to operate, and that in unions with a high turnover of membership it would be impossible to operate postal ballots fairly or effectively. One answer to these dilemmas which is sometimes put forward is to develop the role of workplace-based meetings in union elections. These could increase participation in votes while meeting many of the objections to postal ballots outlined above. The NUM, for example, holds its ballots at the pithead and consistently achieves very high rates of involvement. Another possibility is to improve the standards of *information* available to voters in union elections.

 On balance do you favour the system of postal balloting for trade union elections in your union?

Some people argue that all votes for strike action should be conducted by individual secret ballots, and even that individual strike ballots should be compulsory.

There are several trade union arguments to be considered about this —

1 Part of the information needed by trade unionists in deciding whether they think strike action is *tactically* wise and worthwhile is some idea about how other union members feel — since it is on the readiness of the members to stand together that the chances of success may depend. Some feel that a secret ballot might make it more difficult for workers to assess the strength of their union before deciding about action.

2 Secret ballots on strike votes may prolong and intensify disputes when this is not necessary. The Royal Commission on Trade Unions and Employers associations put it like this:—

'Once a vote has been taken and has gone in favour of strike action, the resulting stoppage may delay a settlement by restricting union leaders' freedom of action'.

On the other hand, secret ballots on strike action might strengthen the hand of the union if they clearly showed the extent of support behind any action. The Miners' union NUM use individual secret ballots to make major decisions about industrial action.

 Do you favour individual secret ballots for union decisions about strike action?

Do you think that secret ballots should be made compulsory by law?

The Closed Shop

The closed shop is often attacked as an undemocratic infringement of individual liberties. It is also argued that the trade union movement would be stronger if people joined voluntarily than if they were pressurised into membership.

In discussions of this, it is important to distinguish between the pre-entry closed shop and the post-entry closed shop. Most closed shops are of the 'post-entry' variety where people are made aware of the obligation to take up membership before taking on a job.

The facts and issues about closed shop policies were set out in Chapter 1 of Trade Union Studies Book 1 (sections 3 and 10). In the context of internal union democracy it is only necessary to add that defenders of the closed shop argue that democracy at work is not simply to be measured in terms of 'individual freedom' but also in terms of the strength of the unions to protect and advance the interests of their members. This argument raises the question: how far can 'democratic rights' include being able to opt out of one's obligations to fellow workers? Certainly, there seem to be few people who regard the British State as 'undemocratic' because it claims rights to impose duties and obligations on people (such as paying taxes or serving in the armed forces) whether they wish to accept them or not.

Nevertheless, because of the need to preserve individual freedom, the use of the closed shop as a means of developing the strength of the union movement does highlight the need to ensure that the *internal* democratic procedures of trade unions are operating in a satisfactory way.

Factions in trade unions

Some commentators have argued that one of the hallmarks of a democratic organisation is the right of members to combine and organise freely within the union, and even to campaign against union policy and the union's leadership.

Unions vary in their attitudes to this. For example, the AUEW has an informal kind of 'party system' through which candidates of different political tendencies compete for union office. One American printing union has a fully fledged two party system, and members belong to one of the parties in the union as well as to the union itself. Both these unions have fairly high rates of participation and close election results. It is said that 'factions' and organised groups may assist democracy in unions by giving members a more clear-cut choice about the directions in which the union ought to move.

On the other hand, some unions reject the idea of factional activity quite strongly. They hold to the view that factions can disrupt the unity of the union and undermine its policies. Factions have been accused of by-passing the proper constitutional arrangements of unions, and of having an unfair advantage in that they are organised in pursuit of their objectives while other groups are not. Some unions forbid direct contact between branches to deter members combining outside of the formal machinery of the unions own structure. Other unions forbid members of certain political organisations from holding office.

In practice it is difficult to evaluate the contribution of 'factions' to trade union democracy. Organised opposition may provide a counter-weight to a centralised trade union leadership. On the other hand, political 'in-fighting' might lead to 'backstage' manoeuvring and a lack of openness in trade union decision making.

Do you have any factions or organised opposition operating within your union?

Do you feel that, on balance, such opposition makes any contribution towards trade union democracy?

Are factions and opposition groups allowed or discouraged in your union?

Special TUC conference on pay June 1976

Relationships between unions — the role of the TUC

Some trade unionists feel that multi-unionism can create difficulties for trade union democracy. In a multi-union bargaining situation, no matter how democratic the procedures and policies of any one of the unions, that union's negotiators will normally have to subordinate themselves to the decisions of the trade union side as a whole. This is not an overwhelming difficulty but it does show that the labour movement generally must tackle the question of union democracy in a coordinated way.

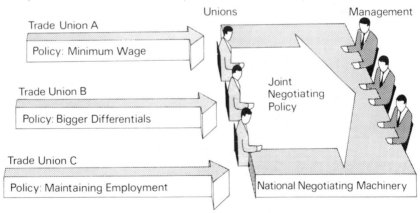

Unions   Management

Trade Union A
Policy: Minimum Wage

Trade Union B
Policy: Bigger Differentials

Trade Union C
Policy: Maintaining Employment

Joint Negotiating Policy

National Negotiating Machinery

Similar problems occur when trade unions come together to make policy decisions at the Trades Union Congress. Unions may be expected to forego their own policies if outvoted by the majority opinion of Congress.

The development of the Social Contract has greatly increased the importance of decisions made the highest level of the trade union movement.

'Not only has the TUC developed closer links with Government, it now has a major role on a number of new institutions; in addition to the National

157

Economic Development Council, the TUC now has members on the Manpower Services Commission, the Health and Safety Commission, the Equal Opportunities Commission and the governing body of the Advisory, Conciliation and Arbitration Service.'

'Consultative Arrangements within the TUC', TUC

Many people have welcomed this as a sign that the trade union movement is able to speak with a united and more authoritative voice at government and national level. At the same time concern has been expressed that developments like this should be accompanied by a developing democratic structure. One aspect of this within individual unions is the development and extension of procedures for allowing the membership to express a view on their union's policies for Congresses. At the level of the TUC itself discussions have taken place to review Congress procedures in order to meet these developments. Maintaining and extending consultation and democracy at this level is necessary in order to ensure that TUC decisions have enough support and authority.

How does your union select its delegation to the Trades Union Congress?

How did your own union decide its policy on the Social Contract?

Did you take any part in the debates within your union on the question of the Social Contract?

Do you think it is necessary for the trade union movement to have policies which apply to all trade unionists?

Action Checklist

● Identify particular groups of workers who find it especially difficult to participate in the work of the union at the workplace.

What specific steps might be taken to assist these groups of workers?

a If women workers are concerned, Chapter four of this book may offer some suggestions.

b If immigrant workers need to be drawn more fully into the work of the union you may need to consider ways of dealing with language problems, and to make special efforts to recruit and organise.

Chapter 8 of the Year One Trade Union Studes book contains further advice on this, and the TU Studies film 'Immigrant Workers' is designed to direct attention to such questions of equal opportunity and to stimulate discussion about them on union courses and at branches (see page 182-3).

c If any members work in scattered or small workplaces, you may need to make extra arrangements to ensure that they are adequately informed of union matters. Shiftworkers and groups with high turnover of staff may also need special attention.

● Examine your agreements with management concerning trade union facilities at work. Do these agreements provide adequate opportunities for the union to hold workplace meetings and use notice-boards and circulars to keep members informed?

● Look at the branch structure of your union. Do the members you work with identify adequately with their union branches? Can anything be done to improve attendance or to make members more aware of the role of their trade union branches?

● Obtain the minutes of your union's executive council from your branch secretary. They may give you a better idea about the work which is done by your union at National level.

● Are arrangements for the distribution of your union's journal satisfactory? Are you happy about your journal's content and presentation?

Are members provided with local bulletins or news sheets giving details of local union affairs?

● Use the materials in this chapter to discuss the following issues with fellow union members

Postal Ballots

The election and appointment of full-time officials

Opposition and factions in trades unions

Improving members' relationship with union work at higher levels

Improving communications in your union.

The film 'Making·Union Democracy Work' could be used to stimulate interest and debate (see page 183).

Chapter 10 'Educate, Agitate, Organise'

A theme running through this book has been that strong and effective union organisation is the key to work people increasing their influence over management decisions. Unless shop stewards and workplace representatives are backed up by strong membership support, their negotiating position in relation to management will inevitably lack credibility, whatever the issue in question.

At the same time, chapter after chapter has illustrated that strength alone may not be enough. It may be sufficient to *stop* management taking a particular course of action. But if you then want to put forward *alternative* policies, you need information and you need to know how to use that information to build a positive strategy, say on eliminating health hazards, or improving the position of women workers.

Each chapter in this book has highlighted particular needs in relation to both organisation and access to information. What this final chapter does is to pull some of these points together and look at what they mean for the development of union facilities both at workplace and national level. We will be concentrating on the following issues —

● How stewards can get information.

● What sort of facilities and organisation they need to make most effective use of this information.

● What back up in terms of research and training they need from their unions to help them in this process.

Questions

1 Does your shop stewards committee have its own library of pamphlets, books, newspaper cuttings and so on?

Yes ☐   No ☐

2 Do you get information from management on

	Regularly	Sometimes	Never
Average earnings	☐	☐	☐
Numbers employed	☐	☐	☐
Numbers leaving	☐	☐	☐
Absenteeism	☐	☐	☐
Sickness	☐	☐	☐
Accidents	☐	☐	☐
Output per man	☐	☐	☐
Sales	☐	☐	☐
Profits	☐	☐	☐
Investment plans	☐	☐	☐

3 Which of the following sources have you used in getting information

Reference Library ☐

Union Research Department ☐

Sympathetic 'expert' or academic ☐

Other shop stewards ☐

4 Does your shop stewards committee have

	Yes	No
An office or office space	☐	☐
Use of telephone	☐	☐
Use of duplicator	☐	☐
Use of filing cabinet	☐	☐
Use of notice board	☐	☐
Use of internal post system	☐	☐

5 Do shop stewards at your workplace have a right to time off with average earnings

	Yes	No
for shop stewards duties	☐	☐
for training courses approved by union	☐	☐
to attend conferences organised by their unions	☐	☐

6 Does your shop stewards committee meet

regularly	☐	☐
only when problems arise	☐	☐

7 Do you have workplace meetings with the membership

regularly	☐	☐
only when issues arise	☐	☐

8 Are workplace meetings held

outside work hours ☐

during work hours with loss of pay ☐

during work hours with no loss of pay ☐

9 Do you provide information sheets for the membership

regularly	☐	☐
only when issues arise	☐	☐

10 How many stewards at your workplace have attended union training courses during the last year?

11 Have you organised any educational meetings or talks at your workplace or branch in the last year?

☐   ☐

Information needs — a review

Your information needs for effective negotiating about the members pay and job security are spelt out in the section 'Disclosure of Information' in Trade Union Studies Book 1, which includes a complete checklist of issues to be discussed at the stewards' or branch committee on the subject.

But this book has indicated a further range of information that is essential for a well worked-out strategy that aims to increase democracy at work. The checklists at the end of each chapter have suggested specific kinds of information you will need.

For example, chapter 1 stressed the importance of having copies of all your agreements and of union policy statements. Chapter 2 concentrated on information for monitoring and eliminating safety hazards, which included accident figures, information on substances and processes used, information on standards and information on management's investment and product plans. A number of sources of information were suggested, including management, the factory inspectorate, sympathetic experts, plus your own library of material on the hazards and standards most relevant to your work. Another important point that came out in this chapter was that in order to get full membership support, it is important that members as well as shop stewards are aware of this information and what it means for them.

In chapter 3 we saw how the monitoring of information on absenteeism and turnover might help in pinpointing jobs and departments where members are particularly bored and frustrated with their work. And once more, as with safety, it was emphasised that in order to really tackle problems at source, information is needed on management's future investment plans.

In chapter 4 we saw that information on earnings, recruitment, training and promotion were the key both to pinpointing the main problem areas for women's rights and to monitoring improvements in these areas. An equally important theme of this chapter was that you need information on women within the union as well as on women at work, in order to find out where women are less involved than they might be, and to work out policies for increasing their involvement and improving union solidarity.

Chapter 5 looked at what is often considered a highly specialised topic, pensions. One aim of the chapter was to show how stewards, by acquiring some basic knowledge about legal requirements and by getting access to essential information on membership records and funding, could begin to develop an effective strategy on pensions.

An important message of chapter 6 was that where your workplace is part of a larger organisation you need to do quite a bit of research about your organisation as a whole — about its ownership structure and about what decisions are taken where and by whom.

Again a variety of sources were suggested for this information — management themselves, reference books like 'Who Owns Whom', and shop stewards at other workplaces in the organisation. We saw that the communication of information between plants on questions like collective agreements, manpower, forward plans was particularly important and that this raised the need for new developments in union organisation.

Chapters 7 and 8 looked at new possible sources of obtaining information, through trade union representation on policy making bodies in the private and public sectors. This raised the question of how well equipped trade unionists are to cope with planning information and whether there was a danger of them being persuaded into accepting management interpretations. We looked at the argument that the best way to safeguard the independence of union representatives was to make sure that they were backed up with effective training and research facilities and strong membership organisation. We will be looking in more detail at the question of training later in this chapter.

One danger, as stewards themselves become more and more 'expert' in dealing with management information, is that they themselves become an 'elite' isolated from the membership.

In chapter 9, on democracy in unions, we saw that an important way of guarding against 'elitism' at any level of the union is to make sure that information is not 'hoarded' by any one group. There has to be a *flow* of information from head office to stewards, from stewards to the membership. Just what this means in practical terms of organisation is something we return to at a number of points in this chapter. And of course the question of training is also relevant here. If *members* are going to play a full role in policy-making then they need training just as much as shop stewards.

 Can you see any dangers at your workplace of stewards becoming an expert 'elite'?

Sources of Information

We have seen in this brief review that there are a number of ways of getting information. You might get information direct from your employer, you might get it through the union structure, either from head office, from other shop stewards, or from the membership, or you could use 'outside' sources such as reference libraries, the factory inspectorate, sympathetic experts and so on. In this section we look in more detail at these ways of getting information, starting with the employer.

Your employer

Look back at your answers to question 2 at the beginning of the chapter. How many of the kinds of information listed did you get regularly from management?

Obtaining *regular* information from management is a vital point. A set of figures in isolation on accidents, recruitment or investment does not really tell us much. It tells us a lot more if we can *compare* it with information we already have on the same subject — for example, comparing accident figures for one month to the last month, or comparing accident figures for one department to another department; comparing investment plans for one year to the previous year, or comparing investment plans for your workplace to plans for another part of the organisation and so on. By making such comparisons we can *monitor* situations — monitor whether the situation is improving or getting worse from a union point of view, monitor how the situation in one department compares to other departments, monitor how the situation in your workplace compares to other workplaces in your organisation, monitor how the situation in your workplace compares to national trends or standards. It is only by monitoring these developments on a regular basis that you can decide as trade unionists on what *action* needs to be taken, on what issues need to be raised with management.

Getting regular information

We saw in chapter 6 that an important part of management's job is monitoring the performance of their organisation. This was what budgetary control was all about — continuously comparing targets with actual performance in a wide range of areas. This means that management already systematically collect information on many of the issues in which trade unionists will be interested. And moreover this information is usually circulated regularly to management at all levels of the organisation through an internal circulation list. One way for shop stewards to get access to regular information is to get agreement with management that they are included in this circulation list.

 Does your shop stewards committee receive copies of internal management information documents?

Has your shop stewards committee asked to be included on the internal circulation list?

Another way to make sure of regular access to information is to negotiate an *information agreement*. The 1977 TUC Economic Review urged that

'An objective of all trade union workplace representatives should be the drawing up with management of information agreements or procedures which provide for the disclosure of clearly defined types of information on a regular basis'.

What you need to decide in drawing up such an agreement is what information you want, in what form and how often.

Working through this book should have helped to give you some idea of the kinds of information you need. The TUC booklet Industrial Democracy sets out a list of information that management should disclose to trade union representatives, and you may find it helpful to look at this. But it is important that you think very carefully about what you would use information for if you got it. There is absolutely no point in collecting information just for the sake of it!

The *form* in which you get information is of course very important and relates once again to what you want the information for. For example, we pointed out in chapter 4 that if you are going to monitor the position of women at your workplace, you will need to have figures on numbers employed, grades, earnings, training and so on all broken down by sex.

Similarly the importance of knowing about future investment plans was stressed in a number of chapters; but the information that your company as a whole is investing say £5 million over the next year will tell you very little.

You will need to know how this investment is being allocated between different plants, whether any new plants are planned, how much of the investment is being allocated to new machinery in existing plants, how much is being allocated for the general improvement of working environment and safety conditions. Only then can you discuss properly the implications of management's proposed actions for job security, recruitment, training, safety, work organisation, job design and so on. Another important point to remember when thinking about the form in which information is presented is that information may not always be *neutral*. The way in which information is presented can to a large extent determine the interpretation of the information. And if management decides the form in which information is presented, then the interpretation might be a management one. For example, look at the following classification of accident information made in a British Steel Corporation report 'Lost Time Injury Statistics':

Causes of Accident

Errors of judgement	3,263 incidents
Unsafe attitude	1,467 incidents
Lack of tidiness	1,129 incidents
System of work	909 incidents
Lack of skill in the job	543 incidents

The information here is certainly not 'neutral'. A great number of assumptions have been made both in selecting the categories of 'errors of judgement', 'unsafe attitude', and so on, and in allocating incidents to categories. The 'message' that emerges from this classification is that the vast number of accidents are due to carelessness or error on the part of the workers. This is a message that no shop steward would want to accept at face value.

This illustrates the importance of getting agreement with management on the presentation of information, and making sure that there is the minimum possible management 'interpretation' on the information you receive.

Have you ever received information from management that was presented in such a way as very obviously to 'bias' it to management's point of view?

Can you think of other ways in which the information could have been presented to avoid this?

The other important point to consider for an information agreement is *how often* you want the information. For example, information on overtime or bonus earnings you might want on a weekly basis to monitor changes and fluctuations; information on questions like average earnings, numbers recruited, numbers leaving, absenteeism, sickness, accidents may be sufficient on a monthly basis. The timing of disclosure of information on management planning and control figures is probably best linked to the time-scale of management's own control system. We suggested in chapter 6 that corporate and financial plans usually cover a number of years, but they are likely to be reviewed and 'rolled forward' every year, and so trade unionists might seek yearly disclosure of major forward planning information. Divisional budgets might be set and reviewed on say a 6 monthly basis and so disclosure of information to trade unionists on both targets and actual performance might follow the same time-scale. Similarly the timing of disclosure on plant targets and performance might be monthly.

Of course it is not possible to set a fixed time for the disclosure of all kinds of information — for example safety representatives will want a breakdown of any new substances before they are introduced. It is no good waiting until the end of the month. Provision for this kind of disclosure could be made either in a safety agreement or in a general information agreement.

As well as needing regular information, shop stewards will often find that tackling a particular dispute or grievance means they need new information quickly. So an information agreement should set out a procedure for this, making clear how a request for information should be submitted, the time limits in which management must respond, and also the steps to be taken if there is disagreement over whether or not the information should be disclosed.

The law as support

Many managements are reluctant to disclose information to unions. They see it as yet a further eating away of their 'prerogatives'. If management is reluctant to release information, then you can remind them that under the Employment Protection Act (sections 19-21) they have a general duty to disclose at all stages of collective bargaining information requested by representatives of independent trade unions. If the information relates to Health and Safety, then you can refer to the disclosure provisions in the Health and Safety at Work Act that we looked at briefly in chapter 2. But as we have stressed throughout this book, trade unionists cannot afford to assume the law is adequate and fully enforceable. In fact under the Employment Protection Act there is no way that an employer can be actually forced to disclose information even after a recommendation from the Central Arbitration Committee. All that can be won through the law at the end of the day is an award for improved terms and conditions of employment.

ACAS have published a code of practice relating to the EPA provisions on disclosure. And although the code itself has no legal force, it is meant to set standards for good industrial relations practice. So it is useful for shop stewards to be aware of its contents and to draw them to the attention of their employer where necessary in negotiations. The last part of the Code stresses the importance of agreements on information disclosure of the kind we looked at earlier:

'Employers and trade unions . . . should consider what information is likely to be required, what is available, and what could reasonably be made available. Consideration should also be given to the form in which information will be presented, when it should be presented and to whom. In particular, the parties should endeavour to reach an understanding on what information could most appropriately be provided on a regular basis.

Procedures for resolving possible disputes concerning any issues associated with the disclosure of information should be agreed'.

A possible limitation of the EPA provisions from the trade union point of view is that employers are provided with some very general reasons for not providing information. An employer need not disclose information if this would be against the interests of national security, or if this would cause 'substantial injury' to the undertaking (for example in relation to competitors); nor need they compile or assemble information which would entail work or expenditure 'out of reasonable proportion to the value of the information in the conduct of collective bargaining'.

But of course it is not only in connection with legal proceedings that trade unionists have to cope with these difficulties.

How often has your employer refused you information because it is 'confidential' and its release could damage the competitive position of the firm?

How often has your employer refused you information on the grounds that management do not have it to hand and it would take too long to assemble?

On the second question, the point to remember is the one we made earlier — that it is part of management's job to collect and monitor information on most of the questions trade unions are interested in. So disclosing the information to unions does not usually involve any extra work. If management really don't collect the information, then it may be that they are not doing their job properly and you should insist that they start collecting it.

But what about confidentiality? How can trade unionists deal with this problem in negotiations? The recent Bullock Report made an important point when it said 'in practice the label of confidentiality is still used too frequently'.

Management often mean by this term that they would prefer to keep the information to themselves, not that its disclosure would necessarily harm their stock market or competitive position. Under the EPA in fact the burden of *proving* that disclosure of information would harm the company lies with the employer, and this is an important point to remember in negotiations.

Of course, one possible danger here is that management may release information to stewards but insist that they do not convey it to the membership.

Have you ever been put in this position by management?

How did you respond?

We have emphasised throughout this book that keeping the membership informed is essential to industrial democracy. If you feel as a steward that certain information really could damage the firm's position if it got known too widely (for example, make-up of tender prices, cost information on individual products) then you might reach agreement with management that you would report the general implications of the information back to the membership, without releasing the detailed figures for wide circulation.

Can disclosure of information create difficulties for unions?

The common problems that shop stewards or departmental representatives can run into over disclosure, were covered in the section on disclosure in Book 1. Particularly important is the problem of *unwelcome news*. This sometimes leads shop stewards to complain that they would rather *not* have had some information. For example if stewards were given early notification by management of the names of people to be made redundant, this might place the stewards in quite a dilemma in terms of whether or not to reveal this to the members involved.

What would your response be in this kind of situation?

Again, some shop stewards have opposed demands to 'open the books' because this can prove a double-edged sword — inevitably there will be occasions when the books will show that management is right — the firm is indeed making a loss and can't afford to meet the union's demands.

Has this debate ever occurred at your workplace?

What position did you take at the time?

The important point is not unrealistically to avoid facing facts, but to review the question of *when you get* the information. If by the time you get the information the firm is in such a terrible state there is not much that can be done, then opening the books won't be much help. But if the unions are regularly getting information on the position of the firm and are monitoring its performance, then they can detect the early warning signs that things are going wrong, that jobs are at risk. And they can negotiate with management over positive strategies to *avoid* collapse or redundancy. This illustrates yet again the key point of this section — the importance of getting *regular information*.

The union as a source of information

The membership

The membership is a major source of information for any shop steward. Information on questions like earnings, overtime, bonus earnings, accidents and so on can be collected direct from the membership — either instead of going to management or as a 'double-check' of management information. And of course the steward relies on the members for information on safety hazards, work loads and general membership grievances. Perhaps most important it is the membership who can let stewards know if agreements are being broken or evaded by particular managers.

Other stewards

Stewards at other workplaces in your locality can often give valuable information on the kinds of agreements they have negotiated, helping you to build up an idea of 'best practice' in the area. This is useful as back-up for negotiations. And as we saw in chapter 6, stewards in other parts of your organisation are vital sources of information for piecing together what is going on in the organisation as a whole, comparing conditions between workplaces, and working out co-ordinated strategies for putting to management.

Head office

Union head office is an important source of information on union policies, model agreements provided by the union, and best practice within the union. Your union should also be a source of help in obtaining information when you are having difficulty (e.g. researching the ownership structure of your company, or providing information about other plants within the company) and in using and interpreting information when you have obtained it.

Does your union have a research department?
Have you ever contacted the research department for help in obtaining or interpreting information?

'Outside' sources of information

Unions and management will probably be the main sources of information for shop stewards, but building up your *own* local sources of outside information can be vital. The local library is probably top on the list here. The reference section should have a number of books that can help you on the law, identifying hazards, or researching your company. We mentioned 'Who Owns Whom' in chapter 6. If your library doesn't have the books you want, don't give up. The library will order books if you put in a request, and by doing this you can help build up the trade union content of the library and make it a service for all local shop stewards.

Many shop stewards committees build up their own library of basic information — union pamphlets, Government and other guides to legislation, newspaper cuttings and so on. It was emphasised in chapter 2 that having this kind of information ready at hand is vital when dealing with specialist areas like health hazards.

Another point that came out of the chapter on safety was the value of establishing links with local people who have expertise in particular areas, such as accounting, or health and safety. Some safety agreements establish a right for unions to bring into the plant their own independent experts. After all, management have their experts, so why not shop stewards?

If you cannot get this kind of help locally, there are national organisations like for example the Labour Research Department that perform services for shop stewards, finding out information about companies and helping to interpret this information.

Using Information

As we have emphasised already, there is no point in just collecting information for its own sake. Information is only any value if you can use it. In this section we look at the kind of workplace organisation and facilities you need to help you get the best out of the information.

storing information

The first essential is to have somewhere to store all the information you collect from these various sources, and to store it efficiently so that you can immediately lay your hands on important documents. This means ideally a filing cabinet.

analysing information

This is a key job for the shop stewards committee, discussing information received, working out its implications, monitoring changes from week to week or month to month.

 How often does your shop stewards committee discuss information received from management?

disseminating information

We stressed earlier that if shop stewards committees are not to become expert elites, then there must be a good flow of information from stewards to the membership. You can't expect membership support when it comes to the crunch unless they are kept informed all along the line. Noticeboards are obviously important here, but full explanations will often require duplicated information sheets or meetings.

Look back at your answers to questions 7 and 9 at the beginning. Did you have regular meetings and information bulletins for members at your workplace?

Or did these things only tend to happen when there was a crunch situation?

If stewards are going to perform all these tasks, then they need some very basic facilities — office space and equipment, access to duplicating

TRADES UNION CONGRESS

FACILITIES
FOR SHOP
STEWARDS

A STATEMENT OF POLICY

12p

machinery, and above all time off for both stewards and members for union activities.

Look back at your answers to question 4 at the beginning of the chapter. How many of the facilities listed did you have? A 1971 TUC booklet on Facilities for Shop Stewards listed these among the minimum facilities that should be provided by management for shop stewards.

The same applies to question 5. The TUC booklet included sufficient time off at average earnings for all these purposes as part of minimum facilities for shop stewards.

How does this compare with the situation at your workplace? Have the facilities and time-off for shop stewards at your workplace been built up through 'custom and practice' or are they written down in an agreement?

You may feel that if facilities and rights exist in practice, it doesn't really matter whether they are written down or not. And this may be true if all the people involved, stewards and management, remain the same. But new stewards might not be familiar with custom and practice; new managers might try and cut back on established traditions, and there is no written agreement to appeal to. It is always the less well organised that lose out in a custom and practice situation. That is why chapter 4 on women's rights stressed the importance of written agreements on time off with pay for shop stewards. Otherwise managers may try and put pressure on less experienced women shop stewards to settle for less than their rights.

The Employment Protection Act has established a legal right for shop stewards and members to have reasonable time off for trade union workplace activities, and for shop stewards to have time off for union approved training. The time-off for shop stewards is with pay, but the law says nothing about pay for members taking time-off for union activities. This emphasises again that the law sets only *minimum standards* and needs to be supplemented by negotiated agreements.

Look back at your answer to question 8 at the beginning of the chapter. When you have meetings with the membership in working hours, does this involve loss of pay?

While most workplaces have arrangements for time off with pay for shop stewards meetings, it is far less common to have arrangements on time off with pay for membership meetings. But we saw in chapter 4 that such arrangements can be very important in strengthening membership involvement in the union, particularly for groups like women who have difficulties attending meetings outside working hours.

Another important area for negotiation will be the agreement of facilities for joint shop stewards committees at *company* as opposed to workplace level. This will be essential if unions are to come to grips with the big organisations we looked at in chapter 6.

Reviewing the stewards committee
As well as making sure of the right sort of facilities from management shop stewards committees may need to take a fresh look at their own internal organisation. For example, look back at your answer to question 6 at the beginning of the chapter. Did your shop steward committee meet regularly or sporadically? It is very often the case that stewards only meet

171

when a problem arises. In other words they are just reacting to management decisions or to situations. It has been a theme of this book that unions need to take a more positive approach so that they can *prevent* certain problems arising, instead of just reacting to them when they do arise. And monitoring information is an important part of this process.

This means that *regular meetings* are crucial. The checklists in this book have suggested a whole range of policy issues that you ought to be discussing regularly in your shop stewards committee in order to develop your strategy for extending union rights and influence. Another key question of internal organisation that may need to be considered is specialisation. Can all shop stewards become experts in areas like health and safety, pensions and women's rights? Or do individual stewards or groups of stewards need to specialise in different areas?

In terms of easing work-load there are lots of attractions in specialisation.

 Can you see any disadvantage in specialisation?

One possible disadvantage is that stewards may begin to 'ignore' problems or grievances that do not relate to their specialist area. They may just think 'That's Fred's problem'. So it would be important to take care that specialisation did not go too far and that all stewards were fully in touch with the main issues and developments in every area.

Even if there is no permanent 'specialisation' there may be a need at some point in time for special 'sub committees' to be set up to investigate and do research in particular areas. An example of this might be pensions, to prepare the committee as a whole for negotiations. In chapter 4 also we saw that some unions had recommended this approach for doing a survey on women's position at work. Sub-committees might include active members as well as shop stewards, and this could help to keep any 'gap' between members and stewards to a minimum.

Many shop stewards will probably find that they need to spend more and more of their time at work on union business. This highlights again the importance of having an adequate agreement with management on time-off for shop stewards, including recognition of the position of convenors and senior stewards.

Education for industrial democracy
By this stage of the chapter you may be thinking, 'But this is asking the impossible; you are asking a bunch of mainly part-time shop stewards to get on top of as much information and knowledge as dozens of full-time managers who have been specially trained for their job and have a whole battery of experts to back them up'.

This is what Len Murray had to say on this question at the 1974 TUC

'. . . the trade union representatives will have a tough and responsible job, and unions and the TUC will have to get down to developing arrangements for assisting them. This will involve training— not with the aim of turning trade unions representatives into accountants but enabling them to ask the right and necessary questions.'

But of course knowing the right questions to ask is not always easy. You need to know a lot about a subject first, and that is why union education services will really be a key factor in determining just how much progress can be made in extending democracy at work.

We saw earlier that shop stewards now have a legal right to time off with pay to attend training 'approved by the Trade Union Congress or by the independent trade union of which he is an official'.

It is of vital importance that the law recognises that shop steward education should be organised and controlled by trade unions, and that employers are made aware of this. We have seen at a number of points in this book that one of the dangers of stewards getting involved in more and more aspects of management decision making is that they can be under pressure to see things management's way and accept management's interpretations of information. That is why if shop stewards are to maintain an independent and critical stance, trade union organised education is vital. The aim is not to turn shop stewards into management experts; shop stewards are workplace representatives and the first questions they will want to ask about any information are 'what does this mean for my members?' and 'how does it relate to overall union objectives?'.

As the TUC 1975 Report put it —

'The nature and function of union representatives is a matter solely for the unions to decide, as are their training and education needs.'

This is not to say that short company-run courses may not be useful to shop stewards on particular issues. What it does mean is that such in-company courses cannot be accepted *as an alternative* to union organised courses. And once more we cannot rely on the law alone. Negotiated agreements on the right to time off for union approved training are vital.

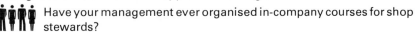 Have your management ever organised in-company courses for shop stewards?

Do you have an agreement on the right to time-off with pay to attend courses approved by the TUC or your union?

As mentioned in the programme, there are many kinds of courses organised by the TUC, progressing from an introductory course to more specialised follow-on courses. Courses are also offered by individual unions.

There are now about 160 trade union studies centres in different parts of the country offering TUC day-release courses. The introductory and health and safety courses are increasingly offered on an industrial sector basis, with close involvement of the appropriate unions.

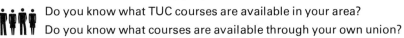 Do you know what TUC courses are available in your area?

Do you know what courses are available through your own union?

Looking to the future

Union education has been expanding steadily over the last few years. But can union education services really meet the needs of shop stewards in the future?

On the simple question of numbers, there needs to be a vast expansion of facilities if all shop stewards are to be able to exercise their right to union-approved training. These figures from the 1975 TUC Report give you some idea of the kind of expansion needed.

shop steward?

or staff rep ?

help yourself to some TUC training

SOUTH EAST REGION
Spring 1977

'It is estimated that there are about 400,000 office holders in Britain's trade unions; if the annual total of student days provided in all union education services were divided between them, it would amount to a derisory half a day each per year.'

There will clearly be a need also for the development of more specialist courses as stewards become involved in more technical areas of decision-making.

But is this kind of expansion feasible?

Finance is obviously a major constraint and we return to this later. Another important constraint is the availability of suitably qualified tutors. That is why the TUC is placing increasing emphasis on training courses for tutors and on teaching methods courses for full-time officers.

Education for the membership
'Employee participation in decision-making must not result in a small clique of union members monopolising information and knowledge, so that the safety steward becomes a monitoring specialist and the shop steward becomes a study expert among many other experts. In a word, trade union education must constantly steer clear of the danger of education gaps developing between union officers and other union members'

Birger Viklund, Secretary Swedish Metal Workers Union

This problem of the 'information gap' between stewards and members has recurred throughout this chapter. The danger is that stewards become more of an isolated elite as their own knowledge grows, so that although they may be strong on expertise, they may lack the organised strength that comes from knowing the membership is behind you and will support you in all your policies. There may be a disinclination to replace any shop steward because of the time it would take a new steward to acquire the same knowledge.

The response of the Swedish unions to this problem has been to see membership education as just as much a priority as shop steward education. In June 1976 the Swedish manual workers unions established a policy that *all* union members must be given basic trade union education and that new employees especially should be given a course of education sponsored by their unions during paid working hours. So far in Sweden basic education for all union members during paid working hours has been conducted on an experimental basis within a few companies in the metal industry, where it has totalled seven paid working hours. Further experiments are to be started in more companies, and the number of hours will be raised to 16.

We saw that the law in this country only establishes a right to time off with pay for union training for shop stewards. So any developments in *membership* training during paid working hours will have to be achieved through negotiation alone.

The Swedish unions have based their membership education on a 'study circle' approach at the workplace. Their new education programme for industrial democracy is based on the assumption that shop stewards themselves have a key role to play as tutors. Stewards who attend courses go back to their workplaces and organise study circles where they can pass on their knowledge to other union members. Stewards acting as study circle leaders attend a special course on 'Planning Trade Union Studies'. The Metal Workers Union has prepared special packages of material to be used in these study groups (most of which are not yet held during paid working hours)

'Each topic will demand 20 hours of group studies and will provide workers with the knowledge and skills needed in order to strengthen the democracy of the organisation, safeguard existing rights and achieve the aim of a democratic, socialist society'.

Is it just as vital in Britain as in Sweden that representatives share their knowledge with the members, and help the members to appreciate the policy alternatives to be decided?

Since few unions can yet afford to provide for membership education, have you considered the ways that the Trade Union Studies films and books can serve as a major — and almost free — resource for informing and stimulating discussion among the membership on all the wider union issues?

Should your union committee take steps to encourage all representatives and members at least to watch the programmes, and no less importantly, to obtain this and the other two books? You will have noticed that the programmes only raise attention to the key issues of debate — the real value comes from going on to read and discuss the book sections.

Could study groups be arranged at the work place, the branch, or at a local college, to view and discuss the films, or to discuss the information and issues raised in the chapters of the books? (To obtain the films and books, see pages 181-3.)

Who pays?

All the educational developments we have looked at cost money, so who pays?

By law the employer is obliged to compensate for time off and loss of earnings for shop steward training, but as we have seen this needs to be extended to cover membership training as well.

Also in 1976 for the first time the Government agreed to make a contribution towards trade union education. A grant of £400,000 was paid which increased to £550,000 in 1977. But the bulk of the finance still has to come from unions themselves — and this must inevitably mean through subscriptions. This applies equally to the research and backup activities of unions we looked at earlier. We often complain about the kinds of services we get from our unions. But in many ways we get the service we pay for.

In Britain union dues in 1974 amounted to only 0.28% of the average male gross wage. In 1938 the figure was 1.5%. So while we expect more and more services from our unions what we contribute to pay for this has in fact *declined* in relation to actual earnings. If trade unionists really want an adequate back-up and training service from their unions, then clearly there must be big changes here.

Certainly, the large scale education programmes — for stewards *and* for members — supplied by Sweden and Germany, for example, are not just the result of the high priority they give to education — their union dues are often over ten times more than in Britain.

Conclusion

We said in the first chapter that there could be no effective industrial democracy without trade unions. Unions are essential to the process, giving working people a collective voice and the strength to back this up.

What we have done in this chapter and indeed throughout the book, is to look at some of the practical implications of what this means for trade unions. It means that just how far we progress in terms of industrial democracy depends on the strength of union organisation, the level of membership involvement and activity, the expertise of shop stewards, the support they get from union head office, and the ability to review and adapt continually organisation at all levels of the union in order to cope with new kinds and levels of decision making. The trade union banners shown in this chapter sum up the tasks of unions succinctly — 'Educate, Agitate, Organise'. There is nothing new about these objectives. What we have tried to look at in this chapter and throughout the book is *what kind* of organisation, and *what kind* of education are needed if unions are going to influence effectively all aspects of management decision making.

Action checklist

● Discuss in your shop stewards committee what kind of information you want regularly from management, in what form and how often, and how this could be embodied in an information agreement.

● Find out what books there are in your local library that could help you in your union work. Suggest that the library orders any books that they do not have which would be important sources of information.

● Set up a shop stewards' library, or review how your existing one could be improved.

● Review your shop stewards' facilities in terms of office space and equipment, rights to time off and so on. Make sure you have at least the minimum facilities set out in this chapter and that this is recorded in a written agreement.

● Discuss in your shop stewards committee how communication and information flow between members and stewards can be improved e.g.

information bulletins

better use of noticeboards

more workplace meetings

negotiating the right for workplace meetings to be held during working hours with no loss of pay.

● Find out what TUC courses are available in your region and what courses are provided by your union.

● Discuss in your shop stewards committee what can be done about membership training at your workplace. Discuss the idea of setting up study circles (perhaps using the films, or using this book) either after work, or during paid working hours if this can be agreed with management.

Where to get advice

on classes or discussion groups in your area

For information about discussion groups being formed in your area, and for any information concerning the Trade Union Studies project — the programmes, the books, the postal courses, the teaching help available — apply to Trade Union Studies Project, TUC, Tillicoultry, Scotland. Or ask your nearest TUC or WEA office.

TUC Regional Education Offices

Northern
Rooms 30 and 31,
Bank Chambers,
51 Grainger Street,
Newcastle-upon-Tyne
Tel: 0632 21725

East Midland
Meade House,
6 Hamilton Road,
Sherwood Rise,
Nottingham
Tel: 0602 606076

Yorkshire and Humberside
Room 16,
Campo Chambers,
26 Campo Lane,
Sheffield S1 2EF
Tel: 0742 27263

North Western
Room 22,
Venice Chambers,
61 Lord Street,
Liverpool L2 6PB
Tel: 051-236 5991

Midland
134 Bromsgrove Street,
Birmingham B5 6RJ
Tel: 021-622 3169

South Western
Guildhall Chambers,
26 Broad Street,
Bristol BS1 2HG
Tel: 0272 20979

South Eastern and London
Education Department,
Trades Union Congress,
Great Russell Street,
London WC1B 3LS
Tel: 01-636 4030

Wales
13 Gelliwasted Road,
Pontypridd,
Glamorgan
Tel: 0443 402677

Scotland
12 Woodlands Terrace,
Glasgow C3
Tel: 041-332 4946

Northern Ireland
TUC Education Office,
236 Antrim Road,
Belfast BT15 2AN
Tel: 0232 749481

WEA District Offices

To obtain any of the WEA's teaching facilities, apply to the District Secretary in your area:

Berks., Bucks. and Oxon
The Painted Room,
3 Cornmarket Street,
Oxford OX1 3EX
Tel: Oxford 46270

Eastern
Botolph House,
Botolph Lane,
Cambridge CB2 3RE
Tel: Cambridge 50978

East Midland
16 Shakespeare Street,
Nottingham NG1 4GF
Tel: Nottingham 45162

London
32 Tavistock Square,
London WC1
Tel: 01-387 8966

Northern
51 Grainger Street,
Newcastle-upon-Tyne NE1 5JE
Tel: Newcastle 23957

North Staffs.
Cartwright House,
Broad Street,
Stoke-on-Trent ST1 4EU
Tel: Stoke-on-Trent 24187

North Western
College of Adult Education,
Cavendish Street,
Manchester M15 6BJ
Tel: Manchester 273 5954

Southern
4 Carlton Crescent,
Southampton SO9 5UG
Tel: Southampton 29810

South Eastern
4 Castle Hill,
Rochester, Kent
Tel: Medway 42140

South Western
Martin's Gate Annexe,
Bretonside,
Plymouth, Devon PL4 0AT
Tel: Plymouth 64989

Western
7 St. Nicholas Street,
Bristol BS1 1UF
Tel: Bristol 28322

West Lancs. and Cheshire
39 Bluecoat Chambers,
School Lane,
Liverpool L1 3BX
Tel: Liverpool 709 8023

West Midlands
9-11 Digbeth,
Birmingham 5
Tel: Birmingham 643 0717

Yorkshire North
7 Woodhouse Square,
Leeds LS3 1AD
Tel: Leeds 23304

Yorkshire South
Rooms 3, 4 and 7,
St. Paul's Chambers,
St. Paul's Parade,
Sheffield 1
Tel: Sheffield 22641

North Wales
33 College Road,
Bangor, N. Wales
Tel: Bangor 3254

South Wales
49 Charles Street,
Cardiff CF1 4EB
Tel: Cardiff 231176

Scotland (N)
Kitty Brewster Shopping Centre,
Aberdeen AB2 3RZ
Tel: Aberdeen 494016

Scotland (SE)
Riddle's Court,
322 Lawnmarket,
Edinburgh EH1 2PG
Tel: Edinburgh 226 3456

Scotland (W)
212 Bath Street,
Glasgow C2
Tel: Glasgow 332-5134

Northern Ireland
56 Dublin Road,
Belfast, N.I. BT2 7HP
Tel: Belfast 29718

What's the next step?

Trade Union Studies Books 1 and 2
If you haven't already seen them, the best way to extend your studies might be to use the two other Trade Union Studies books (to obtain them see page 183). You'll see opposite that Book 1 lists all the main issues trade unions about the economy. Books 1 and 2 also refer all the further sources of information, in booklet or pamphlet form, that the active trade unionist needs.

Study Groups
If you look back to page 6-7, you'll see suggestions about joining, or setting up, study groups with trade union colleagues. This would not only help your own thinking about trade union issues — it could also strengthen union organisation, awareness and participation at your workplace.

Postal Courses
The TUC Education Department, as its contribution to the Trade Union Studies Project, has designed new postal courses to develop the issues raised in the television programmes and the Trade Union Studies books. Further details and enrolment forms can be obtained from the TUC Postal Courses Office, Tillicoultry, Scotland.

Basic Trade Unionism
'But I've never done any studying since I left school — and I didn't do much then!'

Is this you? If you're new to trade unionism — or to Trade Union study — then this postal course is designed with you in mind: 'Basic Trade Unionism'.

There are just five sections, which get you looking at subjects like these:

● Conflict between workers and employers
● Why trade unions were formed
● Democracy in politics and work
● Workers and the Law

Like 'The Bargaining System', it's been designed to make study at home as easy and rewarding as possible.

So it's a good introduction to study . . . AND to the rest of the Trade Union Studies Project.

You can start NOW and it's FREE. (Details from Tillicoultry, address above).

The Bargaining System
The new postal course associated with the first year ten programmes is already available. Called 'The Bargaining System', it has been designed to make study at home as easy and rewarding as possible for all trade unionists, whenever they left school. There are maximum opportunities for you to check your own progress as you go along.

And it's free; all you pay is the postage.

'The Bargaining System' is a follow up to the Year One Programmes. If you want to do this course you should obtain a copy of Book One (see page 183).

The subjects and issues covered in the T.U. Studies Programmes and Chapters

Year One — Book One
1 Organising for the Future
why workplace bargaining now needs to be based on worked out policies.
2 Unfair Dismissal
a general introduction to the Law on employment; especially contracts of employment.
3 Reorganisation at Work
how to respond to proposed new machinery at work.
4 Overtime
why and how this might be negotiated out.
5 Redundancy
ways of coping with it.
6 Health and Safety
what priority for Health and Safety?; what does the Health and Safety Act say?
7 Equal pay
what needs to be done if women are to achieve equal pay and work in practice.
8 Immigrant Workers
how is equal opportunity to be established?
9 Disclosure of Information
what the union needs to know to bargain effectively about pay and jobs.
10 Multi-national Companies
the difficulties for workplace bargaining.

Year Two — Trade Unions and the Economy
1 What use is Economics to us?
why national economic decisions affect pay and jobs and cannot be ignored in local bargaining and union policymaking.
2 Productive or Non-productive?
how the private and public sectors relate.
3 What is Efficiency?
how true is it that British industry is so much less efficient than abroad?
4 The Right to Work
on redundancy, ways of avoiding it.
5 New Jobs for Old
ways of handling changes of jobs with changing technology.
6 The Social Contract
what it is, what are the problems.
7 Fairer Shares
about wealth tax; differentials; and low pay.
8 Wages and Taxes
explains the 'Social Wage'.
9 Buy British!
the issues of import controls and foreign competition.
10 Workers of the World
how is international union co-operation best achieved, and why the multinationals make it necessary.

Selective use of trade union studies programmes and books

If you can't use the whole series, but wish to use certain programmes as visual aids for a short course on a particular theme, these are the main groupings:

A review of the issues on *International Trade Unionism and Multi-national Companies* would use 'Multi-National Companies' (Year One) together with 'Workers of the World' (Year Two).

(The associated international issue of *Import Controls* is examined in 'Buy British!' (Year Two).

Another set is made up by Programmes 2, 3 and 8 of Year Two, with Programme 8 of Year Three; these would usefully introduce a course on *issues about the public service sector of the economy*.

Programme 3 of Year One, together with Programmes 3 and 5 of Year Two, with Programme 3 of Year 3 make a strong group of visual aids on the theme of *the challenge to unions of changing technology at work*.

The Year One Prog. 6, 'Health and Safety' and Year Three Prog. 2, 'Get organised—for safety's sake!', make up a strong aid to discussion and training about the related theme of *Health and Safety at Work*. The first outlines the H & S at Work Act; the second includes the later Regulations.

A course on *new law at work* would use the Year One Programmes 2 (on contract of employment and unfair dismissal), 6 (Health and Safety Act), 7 (Equal Pay and Equal Opportunity) and 8 (Race Relations and Equal Opportunities).

The Year One Programme 5, followed by Year Two Programmes 4 and 5, together pose the main union problems on the theme of *redundancy, job security and unemployment*.

A union course of *race relations and equal opportunities* at work and in the union could be built around the Year One Programme 8, together with the related BBC training programmes, about tackling language and cultural barriers with foreign-born workers, called WORKTALK. The WORKTALK series of four films is available for hire from Concord Films, Nacton, Ipswich. The training manual for the WORKTALK series is available from the Runnymede Trust, 62-65 Chandos Place, W.C.2.

On the theme of *women workers,* there are Programme 7 of Year One and Programme 4 of Year Three. The first deals with equal pay issues, the second with other women's rights. 'What did you do in the Great War, Mummy?' and 'Part of the Union', from the earlier BBC series 'Women at Work', are documentaries about women in unions and are available for hire from BBC Enterprises. (see opposite.)

In each case, of course, use of questions before viewing, and of the checklists in the relevant chapter sections of the books will be important to the effectiveness of the discussion.

How to get copies of Trade Union Studies Books

This book, 'Democracy at Work' (Book 3 of the project), together with Book 1 'The Bargaining System' and Book 2 'Trade Unions and the Economy', is available in book shops. The books can also be obtained direct from BBC Publications, P.O. Box 234, London SE1 3TH, if you send a postal order or cheque, adding postage. For information about prices and postage rates, contact BBC Publications (General Inquiries), 144-154 Bermondsey Street, London SE1 3TH. Telephone 01-407 6961.

Tutors or discussion group leaders who buy 25 copies or more on behalf of a group are given a 25% discount, and postage free, on orders with remittance to the above address.

The three Trade Union Studies Books are also available from Trade Union Studies, TUC, Tillicoultry, Scotland FK13 6BX. From this address tutors and others can obtain books on a sale or return basis.

Some unions make the Trade Union Studies Books available from their head office, at a special discount. Ask through your Education Officer for details.

To inform union colleagues or your members about these books, free leaflet order forms for distribution can be supplied by your TUC Regional Education Officer (see page 178) or direct from the Tillicoultry address.

Tillicoultry also supply copies of tutors notes and discussion group notes, free on request, as well as the research reports on how trade unionists have been learning from the trade union studies programmes and books.

How to Get Copies of Trade Union Studies Programmes

Some of the Trade Union Studies programmes, (e.g. Health and Safety; Equal Pay; Immigrant Workers; Unfair Dismissal; from Year One), are available for hire or sale as 16mm films. The programmes are also available for sale as video-tape cassettes. For details contact BBC Enterprises, Villiers House, Ealing Broadway, London W5 2PA. Telephone: 01-743-8000, Extension 394/5.

TUC Regional Education Officers (see page 178) may be able to give you details of video cassette recordings available at Further Education Colleges, WEA Centres, University Extra-Mural Boards, or Union Training Centres. The TUC R.E.O. or your own union officer may advise about loan or sharing facilities within or between unions in your area.

Trade Union Studies tutors and study group leaders can request any local college or training establishment to make copies of the programme off-air for educational use.

Some Union head office education departments have copies of the programmes as video-tape cassettes. Your union officers should be asked for details of availability on loan for local or district use.

The TUC Education Service has a set of video-cassettes of the programmes, which may be loaned to unions for copying purposes.

Some trade union groups at colleges or other training establishments might be able to use the facilities to make video-cassette copies of the programmes to show and discuss at workplace 'study circles,' inviting union representatives of other local unions, as well as branch members. (See the NALGO example at the LSE, page 6.)

Acknowledgement is due to the following for permission to reproduce illustrations:

ACCOUSTIC TECHNOLOGY LTD testing for noise, page 28; A.U.E.W. Engineers 1922 lockout, page 13; BARNABY'S PICTURE LIBRARY Petro-Chemical works (Trojan), page 36, assembly line (Parker-Hale), page 53, office block (Leonardo Ferrante), page 90, road sweepers (Leonardo Ferrante), page 124; CAMERA PRESS protective clothing (I/C), page 26, Meridan motor cycle workers (Jane Bown/Observer), page 51, boardroom (Mark Kaufmann), page 106, Manchester Town Hall (Ray Green), page 139, shipyard meeting (S/Man), TUC Conference (G/M), page 144; CENTRAL PRESS PHOTOS TUC Conference, page 158; ROGER FLETCHER front cover; FORD OF BRITAIN body deck, testing, fly wheel assembly, gas tank deck, page 42; JOHN GORMAN banners, pages 75, 160, 174; THE GUARDIAN office workers, page 38; KEYSTONE PRESS AGENCY take-over protest page 8, women doing wartime work, page 73, shipyard workers' protest, page 111, demonstration against cuts, page 136; TUC Conference, page 157; MORNING STAR power station protest, page 24; NEWCASTLE CHRONICLE AND JOURNAL LTD Parsons strike, page 21; N.U.R. Unity House, page 149; PACE retirement presentation, page 78; PRESS ASSOCIATION Shotton Steel protest, page 131; ROSPA safety posters, page 22; JOHN STURROCK (REPORT) LONDON Grunwick procession, page 17; SYNDICATION INTERNATIONAL Flixborough disaster, page 34; TOPIX Trico strike (Herrman), pages 55 and 65.

Acknowledgement is due to *The Economist,* 25–31 December 1976, for diagram and extract from article on page 47.

Cartoons by Alan Burton
Diagrams by Hugh Ribbans